IN MEMORY OF
PRINCESS DIANA

In Memory of Princess Diana

Karl-Werner Antrack

UPFRONT PUBLISHING
CAMBRIDGESHIRE

In Memory of Princess Diana

ISBN 1-84426-297-9

First Published 2004 by
UPFRONT PUBLISHING
Cambridgeshire

Printed by Copytech UK Ltd

Foreword

Why is it that people like Paul Burrell, who appeared to so deeply love the Princess while she was alive, should stoop so low as to write a book which degrades her after her death?

It seems absolutely disgraceful that just because this person could not have what he appeared to want in his life with her, while she was alive, should now wish to destroy memories of her; the nation's most well-loved young woman? Even to the point of destroying her two sons, Prince William and Harry's memory, of their devoted mother, who has been dead and buried now for some years.

It seems for too many people (including my wife and myself) an absolute disgrace that such matters, as writing a distasteful book about anyone after death, should be accepted or allowed.

Why does a person, who at one time seemingly having deeply loved another and lost out, has to try and destroy the other person and or the great memory of them? It was absolutely correct that Prince William in conjunction with his brother Harry (who at that time was in Australia) spoke out publicly against Paul Burrell.

This is the man who was at one time supposed to be a friend of the family, when the two Princes were still young boys.

One must always remember however that young ears and eyes are often keener than an older person's and what goes into their minds can never ever be easily removed.

There appeared to be one or two so-called previous friends of the late Princess Diana and seeming friends of Paul Burrell, who think that he was right to write this book, since he was as quoted so devoted and a 'rock' to the Princess while alive.

They are however, in my opinion totally wrong in their assumption, since any person who deeply loves another who is not so interested, will always be a rock, since this will always be difficult or even impossible to be totally removed, without great distress.

And as the old saying goes, 'It is better to be a friend with the enemy, than have an enemy as a friend', since in the end they are out to destroy you. I believe that this can be seen again to be true in this case. Jealousy is a sin as deep-rooted as cancer and cannot be easily removed.

May God forgive the people who have this deep, senseless feeling in their hearts. It is however up to the public to despise these people rather than allow them to profit from such monstrous details or deliberate accusations.

This, my book, is written about the Princess's kindness and help to others, and will naturally not sell as well as giving out scandalous details of her life, but written it must be, to show the well known side of the great lady she appeared to be.

Contents

Introduction

Diana Spencer, forever young, forever loved, mischievous, full of smiles and laughter. The youngest daughter of Lord, later Earl, and Lady Althorp, of Althorp House, Northampton; a very charming large house and estate with a lake containing an island in the centre. This young, pretty girl was born on July 1st 1961, and christened in August that year, at St Mary Magdalene Church, in Sandringham, Norfolk.

Diana, the name of a hunter, was a bonny girl, looking and behaving like a lady from young and seemingly always full of mischief, was hunted herself later in life. She was only 19 years of age, when on the 23rd of February 1981 she became engaged to Prince Charles, the eldest son of Queen Elizabeth II and the Duke of Edinburgh.

The wedding took place later that year on July 29th 1981, when Diana was conferred the title of Her Royal Highness the Princess of Wales.

This tile she held all the years she was married to Prince Charles, until late summer 1996. She had born two sons with Charles, the first, Prince William when she was 21 years old in 1983, and the second, Prince Harry, some two years later.

Unfortunately, alleged misunderstandings between the two of them and some other members of the Royal family brought about a divorce, which after several years of marriage between Prince Charles and the Princess seemed inevitable.

After this break-up, Princess Diana lost the title of Her Royal Highness (or HRH) and from that day she was free to seek other attractions returning to happiness.

Even so, she carried on with her valuable work and continued to be the well loved, most written about and photographed Princess she had always been. It seemed that her heart was in the well-being of every one, young, old or infirm, but especially children.

Her previous occupation was a Kindergarten teacher, and she seemed very good at it, continuously, seemingly making jokes and always full of laughter.

Although she appeared somewhat drawn at the time of the divorce, she always managed a smile, even though she probably just wanted some comfortable quiet most times.

The butler within the household, Paul Burrell, appeared very fond of her, and most likely trying to guide the Princess in the right direction of happiness, or so he may have thought. This however failed, and possibly drove her the wrong way of concern, causing fear of certain people and dates.

In the end, the Princess appeared to have lost her once again happy and splendid life, in a town she so dearly loved; Paris, France, at the thirteenth column in the Motorway under-pass of the river Seine.

There, her chauffeur-driven Mercedes, which appeared to have been chased by paparazzi photographers and others, was seemingly driven off the road, tragically causing the death of the Princess, another passenger and the driver.

Chapter One
(What the Butler thought)

Our late Princess Diana, one of the finest, gentlest and helpful people to others, should be remembered for her kindness to many, including her own two young sons.

That her marriage to Prince Charles in July 1981 did not last, and broke up several years later, should not be of any concern to other people in or outside of this country. Most certainly details if known by one of the servants should never be disclosed in a book, especially in great detail out of jealousy, and in my opinion there can be no other word for any revelation of this kind.

Any trustworthy person, one would have thought, would surely consider the consequences of revealing such details before setting out to destroy their own, as well as others, lives?

The young lady was born in the early 1960s as a daughter of Lord and Lady Spencer, and shared her childhood with two elder sisters and an older brother in the Earl and Lady Spencer's stately home with its beautiful gardens.

There is a lake with a small island; her family chose the latter for this gracious lady, Princess Diana's, resting-place after her tragic accident.

All pictures of the Princess in the press or on the television showed her as a lively pretty young girl, or lady, especially before and during her marriage to Prince Charles.

Charles, the eldest son of the present Queen, Elizabeth II and her husband Prince Phillip and grandson of the late Queen Mother, was well-liked by most of the public. Unfortunately, the Queen Mother departed from this life on Saturday 30th of March 2003.

The year 2003, was in fact the present Queen's Golden Anniversary to the throne, and the herein-mentioned disturbing book, written by Paul Burrell, called 'A Royal Duty', appeared to be once again a somewhat upsetting time for the Royal family, to say the least.

How can a person who was only a few years ago decorated with the Victoria Medal by her Majesty for faithful service, allow himself to be degraded to such an extent that the two sons he had the privilege to look after when they were still young, now accuse him of betraying their late mother?

We can still remember a young and very shy looking Lady Diana just before the marriage to Prince Charles, the Prince of Wales, walking along as a nanny and holding the hands of young children in her care. At that earlier time she was photographed and shown in an almost see-through charming floral dress.

She always looked so relaxingly shy, and yet had the personality of the most affectionate person, which was obviously why Prince Charles fell in love with her.

These two most certainly made a fine couple, and the whole of the country as well as the Royal family appeared a great deal more than just enthusiastic about their wedding-plans.

This was on the face of it a fantastic get together, and a great ceremony on their wedding day which took them in the golden carriage from Buckingham Palace, passing the Queen Victoria statue down the Mall, through the Admiralty Arches, along White Hall and all the way to Westminster Abbey.

A tremendous ceremony followed seen worldwide on television within the overcrowded Abbey itself, which showed overwhelming enthusiasm for the sparkling and smiling couple walking up, and later down, the isle followed by children carrying a beautiful long veil.

With the Abbey full, crowds of people stood outside listening to the ceremony and waiting patiently for the couple to come out again, at which time they enlightened them with the most tremendous cheer.

After being assisted and stepping into the golden coach, both were driven back along the route to Buckingham Palace, with a vast amount of people lining the route on pavements, wishing them well.

This was a fine looking, and thought to be well suited, couple, who were drawing admiration from most of the British public. They would both continuously smile and wave to the crowds, wherever they went together, thereafter.

Children as well as grown-ups loved them both, and in later years all four, including the two young Princes, would bring crowds of people in all countries, that would always cheer in their love to see them all, wherever they went.

Yes this went extremely well with trips abroad on the Royal Yacht Britannia and at home for several years, and as mentioned, they had two fine young sons.

No two people are ever alike and everyone has his or her own idea as to what to do or how to do it, and so it should be. Obviously sometimes these ideas are geared to take a collision course and need gentle persuasion to again reach a satisfactory agreement.

This, which every one knows, cannot always be achieved in a sensible way and many times tempers appear to rise to such an extent that eventually partnerships do fall apart, especially when there is interference from outside.

Every couple should be left alone to sort out their own problems, however deep some of these might be, and there usually is, or can be found, the right solution to stay together and find long lasting happiness.

There is once again an old saying, 'No bed is ever made of roses without thorns,' or that 'The sun has not been made to shine twenty-four hours a day in most places on earth and every day.'

Many couples have their differences in life, but most if not all of these problems can be sorted out with an understanding of each other.

Nothing is ever easy, as once again the saying goes, 'There are hills and dales, with bends and corners on each way, and these we all shall see and have to over-come each and every day.'

Mindless writing about anyone after they have departed from life is not a very good way to pay them back for all their help and assistance, even if one did not always get the best out of someone while they were still alive.

Paul Burrell should have been most grateful to have had such a pretty lively and mostly smiling, caring person as an employer and apparent friend.

As he himself smilingly said on television, he had no intention of upsetting Prince Charles or the two young Princes, (the two young Prince's even used to play with his own sons at times) and Paul Burrell would love to shake hands with Prince William and Harry again one day.

No doubt he would, now that he has lost his job with the Royal household, and as far as they are concerned, Paul is out forever.

It is my opinion that Paul Burrell no doubt would love to wriggle his way back in their favour again, but I doubt that there is anyone whose toes he could kiss to make this possible.

It seems that he has made a fool of himself and his family, his elder son did not appear to look too happy in his father's presence and the public's view on TV.

It is a shame that some always have to suffer for someone else's mistakes, and in this case it was not just a mistake, but a horrifying ordeal.

To place the Princess in a downgrading spotlight, long after she had provided Paul with the privilege of working together after separating from Prince Charles, and her departure from a short but happy life, is more than just shameful.

It always seems best to just ignore a person of such low level, so one fully understands the Royal family's lawyer's feelings, that it would be best to ignore, than to give this man the satisfaction of greater publicity.

I believe that, like many others, publicity and money appears to be all that Burrell is after, never minding the meaning of loyalty, a word his kind obviously have never learnt or found.

It is a pity that loyalty, which we all seek in life, seems to count for nothing once a partnership has been destroyed, for whatever reason.

Diana was a fine young lady who enjoyed life to the full and cared for every one, it is sad that her young life was so tragically destroyed in a car crash.

It is certainly very doubtful – even though the Princess seems to have had a premonition that something like this might happen – that this was anything other than an accident, unless of course, someone knows more than he is presently telling…

Of course, suspicion is nothing to go by, but knowing for a fact that there is someone who knows more than meets the eye, could be very disturbing to live with.

A jealous person might know more than he admits and could cause nothing but endless trouble and headaches in the long run, or distant future.

Let us all have the satisfaction of knowing that if there was someone else responsible for this, rather than being an almost everyday serious accident with fatal consequences, this person no doubt will be found and dealt with in a just manner.

It is bad enough to lose someone so young, active, and helpful to others, but have the suspicion thrown at us that there might be more to this than meets the eye, (without coming out in the open until after several years have passed) is more than cowardice.

It seems that this Paul Burrell was not only jealous of Princes Diana, but may also be jealous of the Queen herself, who he seemingly admires for bestowing the Victoria Medal upon him.

This with hindsight might have been the wrong thing to do, and I believe should be returned by Mr Burrell if he has any feeling at all left within him.

We all make mistakes and distrust can never be foreseen; may that be Royalty or just the ordinary person in the street.

No one in this life can always be perfect, and are able to see through, or into, any person's intentions at all times, however much one might try.

Life and later a marriage, are trial and error situations, which every one must share and respect, as well as work on everyday, if this is at all practicable and possible, to achieve lasting happiness.

What The Butler Thought

One butler thought,
Knowing a Princess divorced,
With any little luck, she could be forced.

But she flew like any pretty dove,
And he had lost her
Sincerity and love.

She was a beautiful Princess,
Who at that time required leading,
While looking like a white rose,
From the Garden of Eden.

We once had a Prime Minister of this very name,
But nor did he
Come all the way across from Sweden.

This Princess was so beautiful and full of life,
Without her love,
The butler thought; he could not survive.

A Princess,
who had many others following round,
The butler realised,
To make an offer he had nowt.

Being full of worry,
Driven round by jealousy,
Following her each day,
For what he could find, or see.

Was she offered more,
From any richer lad?
This drove this man,
Completely mad.

If he could not hold her,
By his offered fruit,
She would not be,
To any other man much good!

He still hoped for the best
And followed her around,
But in the very end
She was not homeward-bound.

By following this Princess's every step
Was no God-send,
Pestering her continuously,
He gained nothing in the end.

Would it not have been better,
Allowing her to find her only way?

When now, they might still be friends,
Enjoying each and every day.

The butler was no good for her,
This she did not know,
He was following the Princess,
Wherever she would go.

And now he's had the cheek to write a book,
About her life,
Describing every detailed look.

Had she but known,
She would have let him go,
Without creating such sensational show.

She was and is the glimmer of each person's life,
And was without a doubt,
The best of mum and wife.

Princess Diana had quality,
To once become a Queen,
And may have been the very best of her,
We'd have seen?

But now she's gone
And can no longer tease,
Allow this beautiful Princess
To rest in peace.

K-WA

Recent interviews with Paul Burrell clearly show the deep love he had for Princess Diana, but he certainly appears to have lost respect for her as quickly as the dear lady and caring mum vanished from life.

All of us know how hard it is to carry jealousy, heartache and deep love for someone who has not the same feelings, but this is life, and we must respect others – however hard it might be to bear at that time.

Trying to destroy someone else's life, heart, love or even person is certainly not the way to go about it, especially after they have left their life under tragic circumstances. Trying to make a fortune by writing a book, diminishing their love and respect is even more disgraceful.

It is all very well for her previous butler to say that money was not the object of writing the book, but because of the Royal family's seeming rejection, which sounds even more distasteful than the book itself.

His own spoken words on interview, saying to the effect of how one phone call from the Royal family would have stopped him writing his book, seems even worse.[1]

In other words, it sounded and seemed that this person still needed recognition, sympathy, understanding and possibly his job back in the Royal household.

He had after all seemingly served the Royals for 21 years, and naturally assumed that he was one of the family, even-though not married into it.

It seems from having read part of his book in the national papers that Paul Burrell has looked down the wrong barrel and shot himself in the foot and possibly in the eye as well – certainly in the eyes of most of the public it seems.

There is little doubt, that there should be a British enquiry into this mysterious car accident.

It has been written, that the French police could not trace the white Fiat Uno, which is believed to have swerved into the path of the chauffeur driven Mercedes. It was also reported that, purely by coincidence, earlier that year, one of these Fiat Unos seemingly collided with Princess Diana's BMW in London.

This once again looks that these cars are not only in France but also in Britain, and it surely would not take very long to drive such a car to Paris and return it to England, where it may be difficult to find in France, or visa versa.

Paul Burrell also reported that he was at that time on holiday in Ireland with his family, and said that every time he made a phone-call to Diana, he would never do it from a public telephone box[2]. What, if anything, had he got to hide?

There appears to be a great deal more to this fatal and horrendous accident in this French motorway under-pass than meets the eye. So far we have read numerous inconsistent reports and stories when seemingly only a detailed British enquiry can produce the actual facts of this very interesting case.

Why does this love affair between Princess Diana and Dodi Fayed, appear to take on a totally different assessment when either written about her by her so-called loyal lady friends or written by someone who seemed to deeply love her, such as the butler?

All the pictures taken and shown in the press and television of Princess Diana and Dodi seemed to show a happy loving relationship, but Burrell is reported to say that she, '...felt suffocated by the playboy's urge to control.'[3]

Could it possibly have been that Paul felt very lonely and no longer wanted to take control of the Princess's life?

Did he at long last feel rejected, and jealousy took over from the previous love he had for the Princess?

After all, as he has said, 'I was there. I saw it. I was part of it.' [4]

*

Paul Burrell is reported to have said that he has not given away any secrets or details as to what has happened within the Princess's bedroom, if he has ever been in there. How can any butler or servant to a Princess be allowed or even think of mentioning the lady's bedroom, never mind anything else?

Especially when on an earlier occasion in his book, he said he placed a note on Diana's pillow[5], while she was out, she obviously did not leave her reply in the same place, but on the stairs for him to find, before entering the room, why?

I believe that this ex-butler of Diana's appears to have had a vivid imagination, which surely put him out of reach with all the Royal family, and no wonder. However as he said in response to writing another book, "I have no plans at this moment in time … I don't know what the future holds."[6]. To me this obviously sounds very much like he has other secrets in his mind or in his head, which he would like to talk or write about. Maybe he will be open enough to tell Prince William when or if they should meet, if it ever came to that.

Is it not a shame, that if meetings with Prince William or Prince Harry, the two sons of Princess Diana, were to take place, why they have to be held in private, especially now that the public has been aroused with curiosity and suspicion?

Hopefully these discussions can and will be made public, or not at all, since there surely can be no deeper secrets, this man has to tell or hide.

The latest revelations in Burrell's book, which I will not mention, will hopefully make the public take Prince Williams's advice and not purchase these outrageous revealing details, which in my opinion can only be written out of spite and tasteless dreams.

It appears that Queen Elizabeth II will stand by Prince William in his decision to have a personal and private meeting with Paul Burrell[7], which I imagine will be to request Paul to stop giving out this continually cruel and personal information, about their mother Princess Diana.

Most of this is believed to be betrayal, spite and sordid muck raking; what has the Princess done to deserve any of these grubby, greedy revelations?

In many people's opinion this former butler is nothing but a brimming, mincing, pouting, preening, and merciless prima donna, and deserves all he is likely to get from the general public and press.

Chapter Two
(Former Butler, Disloyal Rock)

Burrell is alleged to have rifled through Princess Diana's belongings[8]. If so, what was he doing there? Was he searching for possible trophies?

He has apparently said that his book was written in revenge for disloyalty towards him from the Royal family. One might argue that the Royal family have been more than loyal to Paul Burrell, getting him out of court and the mess he got himself into. Would it not have been better to refer to his own disloyalty?

Mr Burrell appeared to be sitting there very smug, beaming even, while being interviewed and sitting opposite BBC reporter Fiona Bruce. At one point, he asked why the two Prince's always listened to anyone around them, especially those who continually say yes.

One would have thought that is what they, as children, were supposed to do, unless it was just Paul who was supposed to have said yes to everything or anyone.

He further continued to say that he felt the boys '...were manipulated and massaged by the system...'[9] it certainly looks as if he does not know, and is just having a guess. Similar to his next reply, where he said the Princes were manipulated by those that did '...exactly the same to their mother.'[10] However, he was not prepared to give any details or names. So does he really know what he is talking about or is he, as thought, living in a dreamland?

Paul again said, 'I would love to explain some portions of her life that I know about. No one else knows. I was there. I saw it. I was part of it'[11], but fails to say which part.

Prince William calls Burrell's revelations, 'deeply painful' and so they must be to any son, whose mother is in my opinion being scrutinised by a rat of a butler who had previously been in her complete confidence and employment for many years.

Mr Burrell, however, thinks that they have to grow up and get with it, saying, 'They're not children any more and their mother will be talked about. She is an icon of the century. They have to understand that.'[12]

One wonders if his boys are by now old enough to know, (and for that matter his wife Maria) all about their father?

If they do not, they soon will find out all the murky details he is supposed to have been up to in the past and God help him when they do. It is never a very good idea to try and run someone down, just because one feels let down oneself.

It would be so much more fun, and life so much sweeter and brighter to others, if everyone remembered the good and best times in their lives and forget the bad or uncomfortable ones, unless these are essential to be broadcast.

Paul Burrell has claimed that the book would not have been written if it was not for the trial accusing him of theft[13], however, in the next moment he apparently says how it will help pay his family's debt, and that he has to look after his family first. What can he be blubbering about? First he has said that he would not have considered writing this book, and now shortly thereafter it is mentioned, that there is more to tell, or another book might even follow.

This might stir up or damage further, this fine young, departed lady's generosity and assistance, which she has given to many others while alive.

It seems obvious to me that this man can never ever be trusted and is cunning; this should be made clear to Prince William before any meeting between the two should ever take place.

Burrell has an old and experienced but confused head on his shoulders, while William is still young and emotionally involved with the loss of his dear mother, whose memory appears now to be dragged through the mud.

It is alleged in a national paper that some have branded Burrell a traitor, whom the Princess hated, and there are rumours that she suspected him of snooping and wanted to sack him.[14]

There are also rumours in the same paper that Burrell may have used abusive language towards the Princess. If so, this is surely not very professional, especially by a servant or butler, close and seemingly loved her? A person's affection towards another can become clouded with jealousy, however, which could rapidly change their attitude towards a person.

There have been various rumours regarding Burrell and Diana's relationship, some of which suggest that conflicts arose over Burrell's attitude towards the Princess's privacy. Of course this is purely speculative, but does make one think considering that much of this talk has come from former friends and colleagues.

It would be of no surprise to expect other stories forthcoming, which no one has ever read or heard before. One can be certain in a case such as this, that there is a great deal more to be told, and the papers will no doubt have more to say on the matter.

One can fully understand why so many people who seemingly knew Paul Burrell personally or have worked with him, seem to have a completely different story to tell now, particularly if money is involved...

Of course, many will not have heard of this man until he was picked up by the police for allegedly taking some of the Princesses belongings after her tragic accident, and its sensational collapse of the trial against him after intervention by the Queen. It was in my opinion at this time, that there was more to come from this particular person; I felt there was something untrustworthy in his manner.

I would like to note that much of what I have written within this book in regard to the Royal Family, I wrote in one of my earlier books, called *The Golden Crown*, when I was happy to forward one to her Majesty and family, who kindly replied from Balmoral Castle. The letter thanked myself for the thought of her in the years from 1953 till the Golden Anniversary of Her Majesty's Coronation back in 2003, which was much appreciated.

I very much doubt that there will be any thank you letter, coming from the lips of her Majesty or any of the Royal family in regard to Paul Burrell's book, called *A Royal Duty*.

As Prince William rightly stated, this book about his mother is 'a cold and overt betrayal' and followed on by saying, 'it would mortify our mother if she were alive today.'

Burrell and others have commented on how Diana's life is a part of history, and how it needs to be recorded, but one might ask, for whom?

There seems to be little history in running any individual person into the ground, upsetting their young family while they are still alive, and she, poor lady, has only just lost her young life through no fault of her own, which every one in this country and others can still remember.

It is hard to believe this person who has written these latest revelations about the Princess, could ever have been a 'rock', as he called himself. In my opinion he appears greedy and manipulative.

He keeps on saying why don't you all read the book first before judging, but is there really any need to fill his pockets and give him the satisfaction of profiting from someone else's misfortune?

Treat no one like Dirt

There is no need to treat anyone like dirt,
Even if they are down and out with only a shirt.

Here was a beautiful, helpful and pretty Princess,
Who had everything, one could wish to possess.

She was a fine upstanding lady and very kind,
To every one, that she could possibly find.

She seemed to go out of her way,
Helping someone each and every day.

There's surely no need, after her death, to run her down,
Trying to do this can be called, no more than a clown.

In this new book, someone treats her like dirt,
When previously, he with her, wanted to flirt.

But she had more sense and rejected in fear,
That he would come close and maybe too near.

His passion drove him in the very end,
To be spiteful to her and no longer a friend.

K-WA

It is a great shame that someone who has had the wonderful opportunity to know and work with this fine, upright and caring Princess, is trying to diminish this young life, when after her unfortunate fatal car accident, she is no longer available to defend herself.

I find it difficult to believe that anyone in this country or the world over would ever have believed someone could or would ever betray the sincerity and love she had for many people, rich or poor, in sickness and in health.

I, as many others, have had the pleasure of hearing, and seeing this young lady just before her engagement to Prince Charles of Wales, at a time when she was a very pretty nineteen-year old kindergarten teacher, and the rest of her life and career from then on until the end. This I found very interesting, since I have always been a fan of the Royal family from the time I returned to this country from the USA back in 1946.

My dear wife's heart and soul is and has been British from the day she was born and followed the Royal Family's travels whenever she could; in the papers and later on television, to a point that I just had to follow and myself became very interested.

I found after taking down notes and studying, that the British Royal Family seemed one of the finest, best known and liked the world over.

They appear to me, to be the only ones – especially previously with the Queen Mother and now with Queen Elizabeth II, her eldest daughter as head of the Commonwealth – to care for others in any country and of any colour.

It seemed this was very much the same and possibly more so with Princess Diana, who seemed a very caring person for young and old, black or white, seriously ill or not, rich or poor; she appeared to have a smile and time for everyone.

Even when her two sons were still very young and she and her husband, Prince Charles, were away on tour, Diana was always keen to get back home to embrace and cuddle her two boys with a happy welcome smile.

But this did not end with her own children, others, if they were ill or were injured, such as the Angola landmine victims, were also shown her care and compassion.

Despite following the Princess's moves where possible during the past years on television or in the newspaper, I only had the pleasure of seeing and meeting up with her personally some years ago back in Zimbabwe, on one of her returns from Mozambique, but unfortunately not to speak or talk with her.

Two African lady teachers and myself just came out of the Christmas Pass Hotel, Mutare, Zimbabwe, after an early lunch.

This hotel was a fine old Victorian style building just outside Mutare town in the eastern part of Zimbabwe, set in a cave-like, mountain-rock cut out, just off the main road to Harare, Zimbabwe.

The Princess, arriving in a small convoy of cars and smiling and chatting happily was almost unrecognisable, accompanied by her friends and bodyguards. The visit was completely out of the blue, without any news or knowledge, to us at least.

At that time I did not take a great deal of notice, since I knew she was in Mozambique, a country joining up with Zimbabwe in the east, on the other side of the Vumba Mountains, and situated alongside the large Indian Ocean.

This Christmas Pass Hotel stands near or just off the main road from Mutare to the capital of Harare, and the Princess and her followers were seemingly having a break after coming through the border from Mozambique.

It was not until later, when shown on TV and written about with her pictures in the Zimbabwean papers, that I realised it had been Princess Diana, or I certainly would have had the camera and a few words ready for this fine lady.

She with her party seemingly later stopped at the Sheraton Hotel, outside the city of Harare, after coming from Mozambique for the return flight to London. All the people of Zimbabwe who happened to see her or had known her coming were crowding round her with cheers, flowers and best wishes. However, nothing was mentioned or seen of His Highness the President of Zimbabwe, Robert Mugabe, and neither did he seem to be among the crowd.

I wish I had know of her arrival at that time, and maybe even I would have had a chance of meeting this fine smiling Princess for a short conversation and even a personal photo.

This however was not to be and provided me with no bad feeling, like some people appear to have presently; shame on them.

Chapter Three
(Rumours of the Year)

It seems to me that a person should not use their own intimate knowledge of another to profit, particularly when that knowledge was given in confidence. Mr Burrell is now rumoured to want to leave the UK over the furore surrounding his revelations, but surely he must have realised the implications of publishing a book such as *A Royal Duty*? Maybe this is why he is said to be proposing to have a mansion built in the United States of America, near the Disney World, Florida, in the hope of avoiding a backlash in this country.[15]

No doubt many people in this country including the Royal family would be only too pleased to see him go should he make it that far?

I should hope he is not going to spend all the money, though, that he has been promised before he gets it, since mud throwing can often take a course for the worse and may return to stick.

It may be that he himself knows that some people will be scrutinising his book to the last detail, and he is fearing any further repercussions that could be directed towards himself. A life on the other side of the Atlantic must therefore be very tempting right now.

Since most of the allegations and scurrilous disclosures within his book are no doubt from his own memory, often with only his word to go by, he may well have left himself open for scrutiny.

If Mr Burrell is trying to obtain for himself a luxurious lifestyle like that of Diana's family, he should realise there are far more credible ways to go about it.

Although Burrell has said along the lines of that Princess Diana was very unique but completely misunderstood, and that we can hear her voice through the book, one would presume that most people can remember and appreciated her voice when she was still alive, without all these revelations.

Reality is what I feel matters in this life and sensationalism likely to have been brought about through jealousy and contempt.

Paul Burrell himself has said in earlier reports how he promised never to write about the Princess, but was to follow on by saying how his reputation has been ruined and that he was determined to set the record straight. But personally I find it hard to see the relevance here, and how most of the contents of the book relating to the Princess's private affairs should relate to his reputation.

He followed on by adding how his name had been trashed and the hell his family was put through, one cannot help but think how the publication of his book could only inflame things further.

He went on saying, 'William and Harry have nothing to fear from me – neither does the queen'[16]. Considering how he has gone back on his word in other respects though, it is hard to believe him here.

Going by his last sentence, in regard to a sexual incident involving a member of the Royal family, he replied, 'I really don't want to discuss it ... it's not very pleasant.'[17] One wonders then how much he really does know, or maybe it is his intention to make one think he knows a great deal on this subject.

No one in this world is perfect and everyone makes mistakes, but when these are intentional, especially to ruin someone's reputation, this can no longer be considered to be fair or mistaken.

Love is a strange thing and no one who has never experienced it, or made it last, has really a right to talk or write about it. Love is a strange but exciting experience and what one makes of it through the years, not what one dreams of, especially when this seems only to be connected with flirtations or sex, which no doubt is a nice experience to all, but not reality.

But real love and caring for someone, is very much deeper than just physical connections one dreams of, although the meaning of this appears to have in this last century, (or so most think) changed.

Consider the old saying, 'Love thy neighbour', means care and look after them as you would wish to be looked after yourself, not crawl into their beds, unless you have none of your own, of course! One should always remember another old saying, 'Do not throw stones if you live in a glasshouse yourself', since recoils or ricochets, might occur. And one should never forget that, 'Life is not always a bed of roses', they very often have thorn's attached to their stems, which could be more than just prickly and could even cause injury to sensitive parts of the body.

Chapter Four
(The Couple Risks)

Princess Diana in her early years, then called Lady Diana, seems to have been quite a challenge and rather mischievous.

In an attempt to delay her bedtime as a little girl, she even locked her nanny in her bathroom, where her nanny would have to wait, fuming, until Lord Althorp rescued her when he came upstairs to bid the children goodnight.

Many young children have and play their own little games and tricks, for a laugh, which does not always turn out to be too funny for their elders, especially when there is work to be done, but most of us have played certain games or tricks, which we thought was for a laugh and enjoyed ourselves doing it without a further thought. This alone however shows that this young lady had a good sense of humour even in her youth, which she obviously kept through life.

Diana seemingly was a great mimic, and appears to have said in a 'Queen Victoria' voice, to the Reverent Tony Lloyd, 'There is a great deal more to being a monarch than just smile,' which made every one laughed out loud at the time.

She apparently took her work very seriously, but seems to have been always cracking jokes, with her staff and people around.

At one time, when asked after a swim, 'How do you manage to get all this chlorine out of your hair and keep it so nice and clean,' she appears to have replied along the lines of, 'Have you never heard of shampoo?'

When a guest at a dinner party said to the Princess, 'I know you don't like dogs.' she replied, 'It's not dogs I don't like; it's corgis. They get the blame for all the farts.'[18]

Someone else once asked the Princess if she had had her nose redone? When she replied laughingly, 'If I had my nose redone, would you honestly think, I would have chosen this one?'

Another time while Prince Charles was having a nap during their honeymoon cruise on Britannia, Diana visited the officers-mess and found herself surrounded by towel-clad men, fresh out of the shower. An anxious officer spotted her and said, 'You should not be in here Ma'am,' when she laughingly replied, 'It's all right sir, I am a married woman now.'

If anything unfortunate or funny happened in front of her while on a visit, she often let out a hoot of laughter and clapped her hands in glee.

This Princess as often seen on television and in newspapers obviously was a person full of life, enjoyed every minute and no doubt made the most of it while she was still happily alive.

There must have been, and no doubt was, certain tragedies and moments of anguish, but she seldom showed any sign of these.

As a whole she was always pleasant, smiling and caring to everyone she met or ran into, on her many walks on the streets, or her travels with her husband Prince Charles or later on her own.

The divorce from Prince Charles was, it seemed at that time not really wanted, but I imagine forced upon her by unforeseen and uncomfortable circumstances.

But, whatever these might have been, no one really should speculate, just for the sake of arriving at the wrong judgement.

These two people were surely made and greatly cared for each other at the time they decided to spend their life together and neither it seems really forgot each other while at least part of their love, especially for their boys remained.

We all take chances in our lives, which are not always appreciated by our partners or for that matter other people around us, but often it is the only way.

Prince Charles always took great risks with his Polo playing and from the occasional fall from his horse, something not recommended by many of the general public or some of the Royal family, and one would suppose even by his own wife, who looked very disturbed on occasions.

Princess Diana took her chances by visiting and very often associating, or even at times touching, some of the severely ill, like people with leprosy or those severely infected with Aids. We the public, very often take too much for granted or on the other hand are far too often afraid of certain illnesses or even tiny creatures, like spiders or mice.

Although caution is at all times advisable, being wrapped up in cotton wool can be just as dangerous as taking a chance. Where would society be to day if certain people had not risked their lives for the sake of others?

As mentioned before, 'None of us are perfect, but some are less perfect than others'. Taking risks is not always as bad as it sounds; although on the other hand it can turn out to be dangerous, but no one ever knows until these risks or chances have been taken.

The Road

'No road is ever quite straight forward,
There are ups and downs with hills and dales,
Rivers, even oceans to be crossed
In the early days with ships and sails'.

All these were risks, since no one,
would ever have found out,
Without taking chances in climbing,
sailing or wandering about.

Everyone now and again,
has to risk his or her own life,

Giving some a chance,
for others to survive.

There is a road to riches,
which could be very nice,
Or a road to ruin,
which for most would be a surprise.

K-WA

It may well have been very hard for both to remember the good times they shared, in those days, especially with television and the press continually digging for news and later trying to blame one or the other for the break-up.

Everyone, whoever had the misfortune to have landed themselves in the same position, no doubt will remember the bad or good times with hindsight.

Unfortunately not every couple appears to be made for each other, when in many cases difficulties show themselves, but often can be overcome. In some cases no doubt separation is the only way that happiness for one or both can be retained.

This may well have been the case with Charles and Diana; it seems however to many people at least, that there was still sadness and love at times showing for each other in both their eyes, which should never be forgotten.

It has been written, among other stories, that Princess Diana had several men following her. But considering the source of this information I find it difficult to accept.

The divorce must have been very hard for Diana to bear, especially with the two growing boys, whom she adored. It seems, though, that after a short period of deep thought and relentless struggle with sleepless nights on no doubt many occasions, without help or assistance from the right person, Diana appeared to have pulled herself together and found her self-confidence, continuing to pull the crowds wherever she went.

Her main thoughts always appeared to be with the terminally ill or severely wounded, especially children. Her hospital visits seemed to have been her priority from the beginning, with no one being able to stop her.

If all this helped to strain the relationship between herself and Charles, no one will ever know, but if this was part of the course that led to the Princess's early departure from life, it seems tragic it could not have been avoided.

One wonders if there are certain revelations that may come to the forefront, which have so far not been thought about, but these must be fact and not fiction.

The book about Diana by her former butler, Paul Burrell, will now come to be read and no doubt examined in detail by many who would dearly have loved for the Princess still to be among us including ourselves.

However since there is nothing that can be done to bring this young woman back to life, which will for many people be a sad story, books such as this will unfortunately be providing what some consider 'the facts'. I just hope that if there is anyone around who knows more than what has been published to date, that they should be found and questioned in detail as soon as possible for the sake of the general public and Royal family's satisfaction.

Most people who were fond of Princess Diana – and there are many of them around the world – will always remember her for the good she did and brought to people, in agony and hardship.

Although she may not have had time in her short life to rectify all her major concerns or wrong doings by others, she tried her very best during the time she was with us, which did not always suit governments or officialdom. The Princess, with her efforts, travelled to and through many parts of Africa such as Angola, Mozambique and others, to try and find out a great deal about these seriously dangerous land mines left lying after wars or conflicts, and tried hard to stop their continual production.

These mines left lying around under the surface, unknown to anyone, have crippled many. Victims often include curious little children trying to dig them up or even just walking over them when playing.

We have both had the luck or fortune to travel, and have used this mostly to travel around southern Africa, myself in particular. I have had the privilege with my own business connections, although I never managed to go as far north as Angola.

South Africa and Zimbabwe were the countries my company was dealing with, but Namibia, Botswana in the west as well as Mozambique, Malawi and Zambia in the east and north were also visited at times.

My wife and I, as said before, both liked the Princess and her activities, trying to help wherever she could, as well as the Royal family as a whole, and have many friends, black and white – if one can so easily make this distinction. There are many people, not as black or white as often thought, similar to black print on white paper, which is not always so exact, and sometimes one should not try to make such a division. We all have come out of one pot – or perhaps better-said tummy – and when young or newly born colour does not appear to play any role and is certainly not recognised by youngsters. This only appears to matter to some, when people get older, and divisions seem to be created by certain grownups. Would it not be a great idea if we were all colour blind, when we could all live together as one great big family, maybe not necessarily under one roof, but within one world as friends and neighbours?

Many of the present and past upheavals could possibly have been avoided, when so far only hate or split ups, appear to have been created, which has done the world as a whole no good whatsoever. Allow us all to shake hands once again as was tried two centuries ago, not as currently taking by the rich and hardly allowing the poor to survive, is of no use to any of us.

Princess Diana was one of those persons who had in most peoples' opinion only good in her heart and tried her very best to create a world of happiness and healing, with satisfaction for all not only the rich.

She tried hard and did her utmost, but did not have the time to succeed in getting rid of these treacherous land mines, which she desperately wanted to do.

Chapter Five
(The White Rose)

Would or could it be possible, that her fatal car accident was related or had to do anything with her cause against land mines? No one will ever know or find out, but many conspiracy theorists will no doubt cast their opinions.

One begins to wonder there is a great deal of money made out of the production of war materials, and that those who produce the largest amount like the Americans, and others, may have been very much against the Princesses plans from the beginning.

Could it be a good thing or worthwhile to have this matter looked into or investigated again, since this suggestion, or could it just be another unfounded allegation? As the saying goes, 'No leaf should be left unturned'; at least not until the truth of this matter has been fully investigated and established.

I cannot help but feel that any investigation will turn out very similar to the recent one about the death of Dr David Kelley, and the war on Iraq – very much a white wash.

Although all these investigations are supposed to be independent, they never are, it is once again a matter of who, you know, and not what you know, pick the right person and you are in the clear, however wrong you might be.

The White Rose

Some roses are coloured gold,
Yellow, pink or red,
There are certain precious roses
One will not forget.

There's the previous white rose
Of England or Yorkshire,
But there was a 'White Rose',
Which is no longer here.

Princess Diana,
Was the 'White Rose' so named,
Who married Prince Charles,
But was later shamed.

They had two sons,
Prince William and Harry,
With all she was,
so very happy and merry.

Charles and Diana began to sour,
Although full of hope,
But in the end,
They could no longer cope.

They went separate ways,
But began full of cheer,
Princess Diana, this white rose,
Is now no longer here.

There are many people, who loved her,
But some carried spite,
Like the 'War of the Roses',
Who's wrong and who's right?

Love must prevail,
Which would have in this precious case,
Please let this 'White Rose' rest,
In her chosen place.

K-WA

Princess Diana most certainly was the White Rose of England or Britain, which sparkled all the way around the globe wherever she went.

Every one appeared to have adored her, especially children and visa versa. She loved children of all ages, but never forgot the old and infirm – this person was one in a million, with a care and thought for everyone. It seemed to have mattered little, what colour, age or sex; she was there for all.

There are, some quite good phrases, previously mentioned in the press and/or on TV, which would do well, repeating. Someone called her 'A mum in a million', as dedicated as she was to her royal duties, but Diana was first and foremost a mother to her two sons, Prince William and Harry. Others were, 'Diana lends a helping hand as a working woman', and 'What better than the picture with the little dark girl in Angola who had lost her leg in a land mine disaster, stroking and smiling with her'.

Also, when she visited an old lady of 82, in St John's Hospice, St Johns Wood, London, just before she died in July – shortly before Princess Diana lost her own life – the lady said 'Diana is a memory always treasured'. Especially when this lady told Diana that her son Prince Harry looked just like Henry VIII, the Princess seems to have burst out laughing, saying, 'I hope he does not have as many wives'. The Princess made this poor old lady happy at the end of her life as she struggled against cancer.

One time a lady at the age of 65 came along, visiting her husband in hospital. She remembered when a woman turned round, shook her hands, and said, 'Hello I am Diana', which was totally unexpected. The lady remarked, 'I was completely over the moon, when Diana touched my hands to say hello.' The old lady, her husband and Diana are then reported to have sat down on his little bed and chatted as naturally as friends and shared a box of chocolates.

And there was also little Charlene Day, who was so desperate to see Diana, that she went to find the Princess, while she was still attached to her mobile drip.

Charlene managed to have a photo taken by her own mum Diane, while placing her little arm round the Princess, and later said full of smiles, 'Among many photos I treasures this one the most.'

Even on a walk about, Diana always made a beeline for any child in a crowd touching their hands or faces. This she enjoyed most, even though she was always smiling and very pleasant to all. Many people often stood out in sunshine or rain, sometimes for hours, just to see the Princess.

Once in Jaywick, Essex, back in 1989, a lady from Colchester was standing with her six month-old-son, Shaun, perched on a row of iron railings as the Princess left Malcolm Sargent House.

As soon as she saw little Shaun, she came across to see him, the lady said, 'She had this tremendous love for children, it really seemed a great privilege for her to meet so many on her walks and visits,' there are so many one could mention.

Many have been forgotten while others stick in one's mind, the number of cuts and snaps that will be kept and treasured for years must be innumerable.

After the poor beautiful upright and caring Princess Diana's departure from this life through that fatal car accident, there seemed to be nothing but sympathy for the loss of a 'sparkling diamond' from this earth.

This nation has lost one of the finest, sincere, kind and forever smiling ambassadors that it could ever have had. She had her own country and many others, especially the poor and helpless, at her feet just waiting for a visit from her, full of smiles, her care, kind, and gentleness.

Her forever-glowing face was enough to bring people in the thousands upon the streets, wherever she might have been going.

Some recorded messages of sympathy, from British people:

'Your smile will always be with us.'
'Death is not the end of the road.'
'Your love and compassion for people will never be forgotten.'
'You were a very special person and you will always be missed.'
'A lady who brought love and happiness to this world.'
'We all wish you were still here.'
'William and Harry, you have lost your mum, but she is now at peace.'
'Heaven has gained, but we're all left with broken hearts.'
'Now a diamond in the sky, but never forgotten.'
'You now have peace and hope you'll find happiness in Heaven.'
'A pure English rose with a light turned off, but your love goes on.'
'The most precious jewel was Di, on earth now shining up in the sky.'
'A gentle voice said why? Come to us in the sky.'
'Up there is now a brightly shining star, in peace and not in war.'
'And exceptional gifted young lady, to live in hearts, you've left behind.'
'You radiated so much love, the brightest star on earth and now in heaven.'
'So beautiful so caring, courageous with an inspiration.'
'Diana you did so much for all of us, you will be sadly missed.'

Diana

Forget your problems, live in peace
There is nothing to be missed,
There are many you have left behind,
And many you have kissed.

Your world is full of happiness,
Wherever you may be,
At long last, you have earned your peace
To be forever free.

There're many people on this earth,
Who would love to have you still around,
And many love you to be here;
While others, making some frustrating sound.

Don't worry yourself endlessly;
You've been to many, a good friend,
Who know or hope, that all will turn out
For the best, in the very end.

Your boys are here looking for you,
And love you ever more,
And so are many people on your side,
Which you would adore.

We' re only here on this fine earth,
For a short while ourselves,
Just like some fish within the sea,
All have to leave their shells.

Up there with you we all shall be,
Celebrating our arrival,
With our Angel's, and the Lord,
Praying for survival.

When we shall,
All be happier ever after,
With dancing
And much laughter.

K-WA

Some problems appear to have arisen, which throw a great deal of doubt upon this fatal car accident in which Princess Diana was involved. These have little to do with Paul Burrell's new book, but with some luck might throw some light upon this case, and certainly need looking into further.

It appears that a British Investigation was requested, long before the above-mentioned new book was ever written or thought about.

This may have stirred up many people's feelings, when out of the blue came a TV program called, 'Diana: The Night She Died'[19], detailing the events of August 31st 1997, which still appears to have left many questions unanswered.

It appears there is normally a legal requirement in Britain to hold an investigation, in circumstances of this kind, which appears not to have happened with Diana after the arrival of her body in a coffin from France.

There are also accusations that the French enquiry was deeply flawed and not carried out as was anticipated.

Why did it take the ambulance one-hour to reach the hospital? But more importantly why did it have to stop on two separate occasions on the journey?[20]

The white Fiat Uno car, which was supposed to have been in collision with the Mercedes just before the accident, it was, seemingly, never found by the French police. Although a car of the same model was later found, inoperable and sitting on blocks, could this possibly have been the car? This car was said to have belonged to a well-known high-ranking French photographer 'James Andanson' who was later found dead in a burnt-out car in the middle of a field, did he kill himself?[21]

It is said, that the driver or chauffeur of Princess Diana and Dodi, who had previous to driving consumed too much alcohol with medications, seemed to have had secret service connections, was or is this true?

This with the many others unanswered questions, around 20 in all, make it seem very likely that a British enquiry into this accident will have to be opened and carried out, to satisfy the British public as a whole.

Although this whole affair appears to point to an average and normal car accident at this stage, there seem to be too many questions left unanswered.

Was there someone behind it all? A letter allegedly written by Diana, suggests she suspected someone, but the national paper that published the article had to black out the name for legal reasons.[22]

According to the article, the letter was in the possession of Diana's former butler, Paul Burrell. But why bring all this up again more than six-years after her death in a book of revelations, from a so-called trusted rock-solid butler?

Naturally anything is possible and as previously quoted, love for a person or jealousy has no boundaries. It seems there were so many men circling like vultures around the Princess, all trying to get as near as possible with some managing to get a small peck on the cheek, or more attention than others, which was her way of thanking them, but obviously quite meaningless and often misconstrued.

Chapter Six
(Light-Hearted and Sincere Princess)

Princess Diana was one of the kindest soft-hearted of persons anyone could meet, who seemed attracted to every one in sight, taking most things and attentions light heartedly as a joke with a smile. This, it shows many did not appreciate, and seemingly wanted or hoped for more than just a peck on the cheek.

Even now the poor lady is dead, some of them are still proclaiming to have fallen deeply in love with her at an earlier time, (this was surely not unusual) but now appear to try and destroy her sincerity and attention allowed to them.

It is a great shame that some of these persons seem to have forgotten all respect and kindness she appeared to have allowed them.

She was a much-loved person, who in return loved and was concerned about each and everyone she met in the streets or hospitals; just as she was concerned and loved her husband and the two boys, including others within the Royal Family.

Reading too much into, and betraying the trust she bestowed on some of them is beyond all belief and should be ignored if at all possible.

She seemed to have been a very trustworthy person with lots of love to give, which seemingly was too often misunderstood.

Telephone calls and or letter writing can often be done in a hurry every day, with sometimes not sufficient thought. And on occasions, too much can be read into some words spoken or written, and misinterpreted or misconstrued, which in this case has caused a great deal of hurt to the people and family left behind.

If this man or ex-butler really liked, cared or even, as in his own words, loved the Princess, he should now be ashamed, rather than amused, raking up such unnecessary details. These would have been better left alone in peace and quiet, which the Princess no doubt would wish for herself.

Whatever would this gracious lady Diana think about her former butler if she were still alive today? Princess Diana is (like my own mum), watching over her two sons from above, including you Mr Burrell and hopefully repay you with a much heavier medal, than our Queen Elizabeth II, bestowed upon you in earlier years.

Betraying anyone, after they have departed from this life and can no longer defend themselves, is just about the lowest anyone could sink to, and no one, not even many of the general public will ever forgive and forget.

It is my personal opinion that this book 'A Royal Duty' written by Paul Burrell, should go under my foot, and under the feet of the public, never mind about paying for, and reading it and then upsetting yourselves!

Believe in what you have seen and experienced, not what some hard-headed spiteful, individual is trying to tell or write with unbelievable tales after the person is not able to defend herself.

Although having hardly ever personally met up or better talked with the Princess, the Author of this book, 'In Memory of Princess Diana' was written in her defence and taking her as she presented herself to us the public, considering she was nothing but kind, good hearted, caring and very friendly.

This will hopefully restore the confidence of some members of the public, who have been uncertain and forgotten the sincerity to all, by Diana.

While the other so-called 'A Royal Duty' should have been, 'A Loyal Duty' and her ex-butler should have remained silent or placed her in the light her sons, friends and how most of the public would love to remember her.

Paul Burrell would be well reminded of the phrase, 'Mud always sticks most to the one who throws it, when it returns.'

None of us are perfect, but as has been said in the past, 'If one has been thought stupid, it surely would be better to keep silent, rather than to open ones mouth and prove it.'

'There is a lot of good in the worst of us and a lot of bad in the best of us, so it does not behove any of us, to speak or write ill of the rest of us.'

These short phrases should be well remembered.

Or, 'Never speak of the Devil, since he could be with you before you can catch your next breath.'

Princess Diana should and will always be remembered by most people as one of the kindest, gentlest and most caring person, who had been with us for a short period of thirty-seven years in the last century.

My wife and myself will never forget the sparkling smile, she had for each and every one, young or old, in sickness or in good health.

There is unlikely to be another better person with such a wealth of devotion, care and love for everyone, whatever colour or age; people she knew or met in the streets or on her visits to hospitals and other such places.

Even in the pouring rain, having been invited to open a new bridge at Teesside, Yorkshire. Walking under an umbrella with a big smile and waving with her free outstretched hand, to the few people present, she looked as if she didn't have a care in the world, and yet it was just before the break-up.

Every one was amazed to see her looking so happy just over a week after the news was announced about the possible separation from Prince Charles, when she unveiled the plaque for the Princess of Wales Bridge, with open-hearted smiles.

There have been so many outstanding pictures taken of the Princess, by amateur and professional photographers and every one with a smiling gesture, even at some of the worst times in her life. But every one of them appears to have brightened so many people's day, rain or shine. She always shone like a glittering diamond in bright sunshine from the day she was born.

Even with sunglasses lifted upon her soft wavy hair, as on a 'First Day Cover Stamp Collection' with her hands held together as in prayer, she looks a picture of sincerity and gleaming beauty.

Similar to one lady who told me when asked why she had the sunglasses on top of her head, she remarked, 'These are not sunglasses, they are solar panels, for the retention of continuous warm water.'

On one of the memorial stamps printed in 1997 in her memory, (1961-1997), Diana shows the brilliance of a lady and princess always to be remembered.

Even though one can see the darkness of her deep felt sorrow within, she has that sensational ever-lasting soft smile, which cannot possibly be forgotten by anyone who knew, and has seen her.

There are so many pictures one could show to be admired, and no doubt admired she was, by so many, black or white, young or old.

Most people alive today may still have the memory of her wonderful, sincere and relaxed ways and movements among the crowd or on single occasions.

Many will have seen her with her husband Charles, Prince of Wales, on their honeymoon trip on the Yacht Britannia, and later in Australia. There the Prince showed off his bride to the people as he partnered to swing her round in a waltz on the dance floor, both smiling and really enjoying their togetherness.

For many years there seemed never to be a sign of differences between the two, when both always appeared to be as happy as any other young married couple, especially when they had their two young sons with them.

One often saw Prince Charles with the two boys teaching them to fish in the river Dee, which runs through the grounds of Balmoral Castle, Scotland, or Princess Diana teaching them to ride ponies.

These boys were still young and full of enthusiasm at that time, all of them smiling, as the boys still are now; following in their mother's footsteps.

Although Prince Charles is usually smiling or trying his best among the crowd, he appears to be more like his father the Duke of Edinburgh, and many other royal males who appear to have this authoritative look behind the smile.

Chapter Seven
(Dirty Washing Makes Money)

With hindsight, It is a great shame, that some of the royal servants appear to find themselves mixed up in trying to hang out dirty washing, in the hope, no doubt, of making lots of money in the process.

It appears at this moment in time (while writing this book) that Prince Charles, had to openly make a statement in the hope of squashing rumours or allegations made by a former employee of the Royal Household concerning what he alleges to have witnessed some years ago, involving a senior member of the Royal Family. And he is quite right when he said, 'These speculations need to be brought to an end.'[23]

Speculations and accusations seem to have gone on for some years, from some members of staff or servants of the Royal Household, and will no doubt continue.

Although one begins to wonder if these had any possible connection with jealousy and thus, brought down the happiness of this seemingly so deeply loving young royal couple.

It was written in a statement released by Charles, 'In recent days, there have been media reports concerning an allegation that a former Royal Household employee witnessed an incident some years ago involving a senior member of the Royal Family ... The allegation was that the Prince of Wales was involved in the incident. This allegation is untrue.'

These allegations were made by a former flunkey, George Smith, another earlier servant, who claims to have witnessed the incident, but in some reports has been branded a drunken liar.

The former valet to Prince Charles, George Smith, a Falklands veteran, has been previously branded a boozer, liar and alcoholic, who has earlier been treated for alcoholism, and had made 'unsubstantiated' claims in the past.

It appears that our Royal Family is much too sincere and trusting and far from putting these matters to rest with an open statement (which is very unusual), some of the public not interested in the happy past, might just be persuaded to try and pursue these issues, to their own satisfaction

Fully understanding Prince Charles and the way he must feel, it may well have been best to ignore this matter, although one of the former royal secretaries said on television that he thought it a good idea, to speak out.

Allegations of this kind must be very hard to bear and keep quiet about, however many people in Prince Charles's position would probably have done the same.

But there are many people who will read between the lines and continue to pursue this matter until they are satisfied; although many never will be.

Even though it might not be what was expected, and possibly hurtful to all and everyone in the end, it is obvious that some people have no respect for others. The Prince of Wales, even though not connected, will no doubt be mentioned on occasions. But this herein mentioned short episode would best be forgotten for the time being.

There will always be people who have little else to do or have the wrong thoughts in their heads. However to try to cause trouble and upsets, especially when jealous of someone else's good fortune, is more than distasteful.

The break-up of the marriage between Prince Charles and Princess Diana of Wales appears to have been so sudden, that an incident of the kind mentioned and possibly believed to be true by some at the time, could easily have separated what I feel was a close and happy relationship.

That is why a deep-rooted, especially misunderstood friendship turning into jealousy can be a very dangerous disease and can easily destroy the most sincere relationship between two people.

Disproving any false allegations especially when made with the desire to be believed, is one of the most difficult, which has been witnessed by most, especially elderly people in the past and trust is the only thing which can overcome these problems.

Many men, including myself, especially in the army, have had the pleasure or misfortune of having to sleep with other men, sometimes even very close together to keep warm, but no one ever thought this to be of a sexual nature.

In the old days or centuries ago, no one would have even thought of the idea of making such silly accusations, even if these allegations of the sleeping or lying close together were true. Anyone making any of these allegations, without having any substantial proof, should be severely dealt with, without Prince Charles having to take actions to clear his own good name.

Seemingly at that particular time some slight misunderstanding between Charles and Diana, (which happens in each and every marriage) might have given rise to these allegations to get nearer to the Princess than otherwise would have been possible to attract her attention.

After all Diana was a kind-hearted person to most others, and no doubt at all times needed love and attention herself, which seemingly was completely misunderstood, by certain male servants.

Let us all just hope, that most people who have had any loving thought for this nice harmonious young couple in the past, will retain their good memories and allow at least at that time the Princess to have her peace and rest.

Allow all those most desirable and over-sexed males, a chance to have exactly what and when they want it, but do not distastefully try and smear others with your own disgrace.

There are many people still in this country and around the globe, which would prefer, to keep themselves, to themselves or in female company.

In the hope of not having offended Prince Charles or any of the Royal Family, we all have to learn by being taught or advised on certain matters, but sometimes it is not always the way expected. All this might sound like the author of this book is all for Royalty, which would be correct, as one who has experienced a great deal, in his many years, and can somewhat sympathise.

From Dictatorship and Democracy I would very much prefer the British Royal Family than any Presidency or Führer, which are of absolutely no use to any country.

Most Royal Families are not a great deal better than some Presidencies, and in our case have no say in matters of politics, but they, or most, have at the very least left something behind for others later to admire.

There may well have been or is a great deal of money paid out to allow these to stand in the forefront, but how much good have Royal Families done, created and left for us to admire in past centuries?

The present Royal Families, especially the British, bring a great deal of foreign cash into this country, which cannot be said for any country headed by a President, or other leader at the helm. No ancient castles have ever been built and left to nations without having had a Royal Household or Family to have it done and paid for. Fair comment, these have all been built with our, or our forefathers cash and labour, but most or many are still there to be visited by any one interested, often as ancient monuments left for the nation and others to admire, even if only dug out of the ground.

The Romans and Anglo-Saxon's did this, and very interesting some of them still are today to look at or climb round by the younger generation.

These are not only there for the nations who still have them, but for many other people around the world who have not had the pleasure of having them, or seeing these in their own countries.

There has been nothing like this ever left by any President or other leader as far as one can remember.

I often imagine that all they have been able to do is sell off the country's gold and silver, to make themselves look great and wonderful so as to be re-elected for a second or third term.

One only has to look at the nation's wealth, if there is still any left, where did it all come from? Most certainly not from present continual economic difficulties.

Kingdoms or Royalties have no doubt not always been the very best, but ask anyone, which or what has been for the better?

As before written, these have at the very least left behind what had been achieved and created, for every one to look at, admire and enjoy.

Even Presidents or for that matter Democracies have had their difficulties to exist and none as far as I know have left a great name or inheritance behind, only I imagine for their own families, most certainly not for any nation to be grateful or thankful for. Apart from maybe a statue, or colourful displays and marches to celebrate those who have lost their lives to keep them in power.

Similar to British Legion celebrations every year in November, and even these are celebrated in what is called the Royal Albert Hall, London. Once again this is a large hall, built by royalty or Queen Victoria, in memory of her departed, but previously devoted husband Prince Albert, the then queen's consort.

This as every year was celebrated again, while writing this book, on BBC 1 at 9.00pm, 8th of November 2003, with Queen Elizabeth II, Prince Phillip Duke of Edinburgh and other members of the Royal family in this very hall, with the most colourful display. This no doubt has been and will again be enjoyed, by all that go there every year.

But what good will this all do, to those who had to lose their lives and for what. We keep saying, 'Democracy and Freedom,' but was all this worth dying for?

One would have thought it to have been, a great deal better if we, or our leaders, had achieved these two little words, without a great deal of expenditure and loss of life.

Would negotiation and patience on all sides not have been more desirable to achieve this, without killings, slaughter or destruction?

Chapter Eight
(What Happened to Trust?)

Most might be glad to read after all the muck has been stirred up by the media, that Prince Charles has decided to retain his privacy and keep quiet about this whole situation, which is a very good thing, and most of the nation will admire him for this in the end.

Is it however not surprising that (since most of the public, appear not to be in the slightest interested) all the newspapers and media seem to say or print now, 'Leave him alone', or better still 'Charles; let it all drop'.

But why was it necessary to rake it all up in the first place? Is this really the Democracy and Freedom, as previously mentioned, they have all died for?

It surely should have been known, that these persons spreading these stories are and have been completely unreliable in the past.

However most people, and we are all the very same, allow too much trust, which was perfectly all right in the past.

But the world and people appear to have changed, when it is most difficult to trust or rely upon anyone who comes to the door these days. This is a great shame, but as has always been said, the trust comes down from above, may these be parents or leaders.

The more untruths spoken or spread about the better the public appear to like it and take it all in without questions being asked. It has in fact been printed, 'If you tell a big enough lie often enough, people might even believe it to be true.' And this is seemingly now very real. No one, not even our Government, can be trusted to tell the truth and get away with preaching a great deal of untruths almost every day. Also, so it appears, does the national press, which continually seems to print untruths and are allowed to get away with it, since there is no one who can or has the money to stop them printing these invented stories. This is similar to all the advertisements, where every large store is continually swindling the public, by announcing, 'fifty or more per cent off' or 'buy one get one free'. Who on earth wants two or more of some particular rubbish, while lining another's pockets, it is a swindle and no one appears to try to stop it.

It appears, the more trade protection officers we, or the governments, create, the more swindling and robbing of peoples pockets there appears to be allowed. Similar to the disgraceful book writing about an old departed friend, who is no longer available to defend herself.

It is however nice to read comments that point out that there is another, some might say selfish, reason for this concern. If these destructive attacks on Diana and Charles continue, there is a likelihood, or danger of a backlash, which could cause the press to forfeit their right to criticise the Royal Family, or many others in future.

How clever these people are, or have they perhaps been wisely informed by the Monarchy of the consequences, which might follow?

It is in fact high time for the media to be informed, that as a whole they should concern themselves with facts, rather than hearsay, particularly the large-scale propaganda which can send a country into a war-like situation. These points should certainly be addressed, where people should definitely listen to the facts rather than the myths. It is more than likely to be found out that these did not have the correct facts in the first place, and caused the killing of many innocent people in the process. This hopefully will be corrected in due course, although too late, but it is often better to be late than never.

This book was not written with the Royal Family or their problems in mind, these were mentioned in a previous book called 'The Golden Crown', which was released in 2003 to commemorate the Queen's anniversary. This book is intended for the preservation and memory of one great well-admired lady, once a member of the Royal Family, Her Royal Highness Diana, the late Princess of Wales.

This very pretty lady is now lying there buried near her old home; the house and estate of Althorp, Northampton, with no doubt her eyes wide open, giving the impression of the stars in the skies high above and far beyond.

She is lying on a little Island surrounded by still waters glittering in the sunshine like a large diamond similar to the Princess herself when still alive, and hopefully no longer involved in any further scandal.

This country has lost one who was very much admired and appreciated by most if not all the world over; she was suddenly ripped from our lives by this fatal car crash in Paris, France, which Diana may possibly have predicted.

We all have predictions and some of them do come true, or at least are believed to have come true if such predictions should ever occur in ones lifetime, but many are part of a person's belief and should not be taken too seriously.

Chapter Nine
(Predictions Come True)

There is a strange story, which I heard many years ago. It concerned a man who won tickets for not one but two free holidays, which he thought he would use himself, rather than share them; slightly selfish, but everyone to himself. The first time he flew, he was a little frightened that the aircraft might crash, so the second time he took a boat, but while out at sea, an air craft crashed upon the boat and they all went under.

Could the man's fears from his first holiday have then been some sort of prediction?

★

It is said that Princess Diana predicted the car crash that killed her. If this was no accident then one has to ask who did it and if so why?

What about MI5 or MI6 as has been suggested, what reason would the British Secret Service have to act on their own, or assist anyone especially the Royal Family or even Government officials to do away with a quite innocent Princess?

Anything is possible, in this life, especially these days, when money appears to be of greater value, than that of a human being.

As far as most of the British public is concerned, the Princess had done, or tried to do only good for the country, commonwealth, people and children.

This Princess has most certainly placed a bombshell among many countries including America, Russia and our own, trying to stop the manufacturing of land-mines, which are only laid for the purpose of killing or maiming others, and when left lying around this mostly tends to be the young and innocent.

Although future wars and many connected or committed industries would most likely suffer temporarily in the short-term, with job and monetary losses, the machinery and skills could surely quickly be turned to better use.

These companies could produce other more useful commodities and equipment, saving not destroying life.

It is well known that large manufacturing industries have powerful resources and cash hand-outs to play with, but to dispose or kill off one extremely useful and helpful person like the Princess, would not stop the idea of the disposal or destruction of Land-mines. It would surely be known that there are many other people, especially those having worked with the Princess in the past, which would carry on and hopefully are still doing so.

I am sure that as far as the Royal Family or the Duke of Edinburgh is concerned, to try and kill off the previously happy Princess married to the Prince of Wales and mother of two lovely sons, is just too ludicrous even to think about.

Or as has been mentioned in the media, just because the Royal Family is of Anglican decent, stopping Princess Diana from maybe marrying a Muslim, is surely too far fetched, for anyone to believe.

There are, or were many black horses in any family especially in ancient times, but the British Royal Family have moved on with time, and old time traditions have surely long been forgotten. Would it not be a good idea for the media and some people to follow into modern times and begin to think before throwing around unsubstantiated accusations?

Even if the eldest Prince William was to be considered to be chosen and presented with the crown to become the future King of England, he would still be the son of Prince Charles and the late Princess Diana; both British and Anglicans. He was truly born and brought up in this country, he surely would be a British or Anglican Prince and have absolutely nothing to do with any Muslim belief, but remain free to respect it, like all others. This would most certainly mean that the idea of Prince William converting to Islam is both ludicrous and unlikely.

This would bring us to the next question of jealousy by her own servants, some of whom have already shown that there seems to be a great financial gain from revealing large chunks of her personal life. She, our late Princess Diana, was trying to do nothing but good for people, her servants and mankind. Several names have been mentioned in the media of late, none of which appeared to have wasted time in printing further accusations. To try and catch them out and bring them to justice, would without a doubt satisfy many of the British and Commonwealth public.

I just hope that the activities of those who are willing to write smearing untruthful details in books or papers for publication, and trying to upset Royal Family members or others to the point of disgust, will meet some sort of divine retribution, especially those who are now trying to dispose of hand-written letters which in the past seem to have been exchanged between themselves, or handed over for safe keeping.

Those persons now trying to sell these letters for the sake of financial gain, and to belittle a person and her family after death, can surely have little in the way of morals.

Even Yvonne Smith, ex-wife of George Smith the former servant to Charles and Diana, revealed that she often doubted the amount of truth in much of what he told her, saying, 'There have been times when I wonder if he is telling the truth, and is it because he's had a drink or two.'[24] One therefore presumes much of the recent allegations are probably in his head and that he no doubt wanted revenge.

Poor fellow appears now to be stressed, leading to severe depression and breakdown about this sex-scandal, which seems to have done him no good at all.

Princess Diana, most likely and completely unwittingly might have fuelled his fantasies, while trying to comfort him and helping him through difficult times. But she surely did not or ever thought that he might betray the good lady's memory by expressing her involvement in these allegations.

Of course it has been stated that the person in question here was at no time in his years of service to bring the Prince his breakfast in bed. His job as under butler seemingly was in the main to lay out Prince Charles' uniforms and decide on what medals to wear, depending on the occasion.

The Princess's fear of the number 13 may well have come from, the couples thirteen years of happy marriage, when servants began to get jealous of each other and Prince Charles.

Every one of the male servants, it seems, wanted to get as near as possible to the Princess, since she was the one who listened to their everyday problems and called them kind names, which some seemed to have completely misunderstood.

That was no doubt that concern may have developed when her husband Prince Charles and the Royal Family became aware of her meaningless close relationships with servants, which at that time was considered outside of the tradition of royal behaviour.

It is possible that Princess Diana, who was familiar to a different life-style of cuddling children and being close to people, did not understand the customs that came with being a member of the Royal Family, and as a result her relationship with Charles broke up.

Princess Diana was genuinely concerned about all people including servants and no doubt thought (like many others) that the Royal Family was too out of touch with the modern world to understand her concerns. Although it is possible that the princess was wrong to allow herself to become too close to servants when many may have had ulterior motives for being close to her.

She was like many other people, including the Queen herself; too trusting and fell for overwhelming charm and seeming loyalty. The later disloyalty shown by some of their servants could not possibly have been foreseen either by them or the public.

It seems however that the Princess found out in the end, and that she felt betrayed and blasted the royal valet George Smith over his previously suggested rape claim and is reported to have said to him, 'You have been lying to me. I never want to see you, speak to you or hear from you again.' [25] This has apparently only just recently been revealed, by one of Diana's closest lady friends, Simone Simmons.

How could anyone fall that low, making up and producing stories of this kind, which must have added a great deal of stress to an already stressful life. Diana had an ingenious way of befriending people and liked a crusade, taking on many cases of staff complaints when they felt they had suffered grave injustice at the palace, which anyone feels at sometime or other. Once bad feelings arise, the rot sets in, and all sorts of allegations are thrown around out of spite to make matters worse. And rather than sit down and discuss these accusations in detail, find the culprit and deal with the situation at the time. One should never allow these matters to get out of all proportion if possible.

It has been stated that Diana could be quite volatile at times (as no doubt we all can) but she loved Charles, and seemingly he let her down, which may well be correct, but one has to try and see things from both sides.

It seems that both or all sides have to take a certain amount of the blame, since no one managed to control the situation.

They no longer believed one another sufficiently to close ranks, or sit down and discuss openly, when the originators may have been found out in time and stopped the break-up of a fine family.

It seems to have now come to light, that Diana knew that George Smith had been lying about finding two men in bed together; one of them suggested to have been Charles, which she is said to have described as, 'absolute rubbish.'[26]

This surely shows that Princes Diana loved and knew her husband Prince Charles, but why did she allow matters to get out of hand at that earlier time?

It would seem that in her isolation, Diana was prone to turning to her staff in times of distress. It is likely for this reason that she became closely acquainted with servants such as Paul Burrell. It is no doubt, as we now know, that it was one of the biggest mistakes the Royal Family ever made; employing a man of Burrell's character.

It seems to many people, if this man Paul would have had the decency not to begin this muckraking, there would not have been so much smell about. As a person who was trusted with some of the greatest personal details of Princess Diana and received her and other Royal Family member's confidence, he now appears to be smirking in the background. He should be made to come forward and produce the evidence with facts and proof of his accusations, rather than be allowed to profit from these.

There appears to be another smug or smirking reporter in one paper who seems to want to rival Burrell, saying there are probably tapes of ever more lurid and embarrassing material to come, and that it is not over yet. One cannot for one moment believe that Diana is proving '…as capable of inflicting damage on her ex-husband from beyond the grave as she ever was when she was alive,'[27] as reported by the columnist Richard Littlejohn for *The Sun* newspaper. Similarly to his strange suggestion, 'What the hell was this Lady doing turning up at the Priory clinic, [or was it at his home] with a bottle of booze for George Smith?'

One must surely conclude from these stories, that this male reporter was actually there and can confirm all the above mentioned, or is this just another unproven accusation, which should be investigated?

George Smith has also claimed he was raped by one of the royal staff. It is said that such allegations could be proved through a tape, which Smith says he persuaded Diana to make of them. Would it not be better to forget all about any of these suggestions or allegations, which quite possibly may have widened the rift between Diana and Charles? What a shame these troubled men were not spotted in time, which may well have had a great impact on how things turned out.

It is my opinion, that the reporter Littlejohn is little better than the people who have served the Royal Family and now try to stab them in the back. Especially when he remarks '...nothing would surprise me when it comes to the Royal Family,'[28] what exactly does he mean by this? Nothing indeed surprises the majority of people about his articles in the papers and I am certain he would be better employed stirring all that is leftover in an army-mess. Surely no one gets a great deal of satisfaction out of his articles, especially when these are headlined, 'Di's Revenge From Beyond The Grave'.

Most of us have our sinister thoughts, but these are often best kept to ourselves. As the phrase goes, 'It is better to keep your mouth shut and be thought a fool, than to open, and prove it'. Why is it that people have to be spiteful, rather than friendly in the hope of being recognised? Never has stabbing a knife in the back of anyone whom one does not particularly like done any good, since this may only return, and hurt you in the process.

Facts can be told or written about without having to turn nasty in the process, which will only turn other people against the articles or stories suggested.

As written on many occasions in the past, no one is perfect and everyone may have a different point of view on any given subject, may these be facts, fantasies or even suspicions.

Even the young man Littlejohn, just written about, has at times written in my opinion far more sensible articles and I feel that a few more years in his job with learning might yet make a man of him, although he does write for a rather sleazy and downmarket newspaper. However, there is nothing wrong with that, as long as they can sell the rubbish and propaganda to the public, and seemingly they have managed to do this quite well, so they appear to claim every now and again, or can this be wrong as well?

In years gone by, these papers have had Princess Diana and Prince Charles of Wales spread all over their front and inside pages, but now other young ladies have taken their place. The Princess was one of the attractions to most folk in her days or years and should never have been treated the way she has been by her former butler Paul Burrell in his book, or national papers, (papers who made a fortune out of her when she was alive), as has been seen recently.

Writing

There are many good reasons for writing,
And one has just come into my head.

It is surely much better to write while you're living,
Since there is little chance to write when you're dead.

Most people would like to write,
But many cannot find their own words or pen.

They have plenty of stories in the head,
But only think of them now and then.

Writing is good for everyone,
Even if many are only jokes.

Often they come from ladies,
But most of them come from blokes.

Why do most parents or papers call children kids?
Most, later turn out much better than nits!

Children are children, girls or boys,
Please do not treat them, as just some toys.

They are, our future generation not just some bits,
Which one picks up out of the gutter at any time?

Treat them like children right from their birth,
They might write about you in later years.

K-WA

I will now return once again to the time when this dear, brilliant, successful and smiling Princess was still alive and with us, travelling around the Globe looking for and after people, rich or poor.

It seems clear that the Princess could foresee some of her future problems from comments that she made while alive. We all seem to have some sort of mental illusion or weird dreams, which very seldom come true in real life, but in this case it appears that they did.

Chapter Ten
(Illusions or Dreams?)

At one time in my young years I had a mental illusion or image that one day my dad was going to kill me after my dear mum had departed, but this turned out to be a bad dream, unless it was just symbolic of that period.

I am still here even though I have at times walked under ladders and crossed the road in front of many lorries or cars. I was almost run over by a US tank, millimetres from my head in the war, and was wounded several times, but was later to survive four years in POW labour camps.

Stranger and more dangerous things have no doubt happened to many other people and presentiments do not always come true, thank God.

⋆

In fact I had a very strange dream the night 13th November 2003 involving my wife and some of our farming friends from Zimbabwe, South Africa. My wife now says that the thirteenth day of the month is her lucky day.

In my dream, we were driving along a strange road in our Range-Rover, when someone said, 'It's a lovely day I would love to go for a swim.'

I replied, 'There are a couple of lakes down this hill, where we have been before, I'll pull up when we get there and we can all go for a swim.' The road was strange to me and yet I seemed to remember the hill and the two lakes, which were there in front of us in my dream.

By the time we got to the bottom of the road, I looked across the lake and there was my wife in a small dingy coming towards the edge to meet us, (although she was earlier sitting in the car with us). As she got near to the bank she tried to get out of the boat, the boat slid away and she fell into the water and went under.

A male friend of ours, who sat next to me in the car, jumped out, shot down the grass-embankment and into the water to rescue my wife. By the time we – one of my friend's daughters and myself – could get down to the water edge, the male friend had pulled my wife up in the water, then dropped her back in again and declared her as dead. We both shouted simultaneously to try and keep her head above water and both jumped in to get my wife out, completely lifeless and all of us carried her up to the grass-bank near the car.

There I held her in my arms, while the other two friends ran up the hill to find a telephone or someone to ring for an ambulance.

It was nice and warm with the sun high in the sky, myself and of course my wife drenched, soaking wet. After some time, she suddenly opened her eyes and said, 'What lovely sunshine,' and laid down again breathing.

I turned her head to one side in case of water trying to emerge, I was completely overjoyed and did not quite know what to do, we cuddled each other and I woke.

After getting up from bed myself, I told my wife over breakfast about this strange dream, and she jokingly suggested I do not like our white farmer friend any more, since he dropped me back into the water and declared me dead.

Continuing to talk, she suddenly said, 'Did you read that story in the paper last night where a toddler was found floating face down in a swimming pool in America, thought to be dead, but later recovered?' This story I had not read or known anything about, but with some luck we still had the newspaper.

The little twenty-month-old girl had been found breathing two hours after having been declared dead by two doctors, and it was forty minutes earlier that medics and police had tried but failed to revive her.

It seems that her mum had found her floating face down in the family's swimming pool, in California, America. Luckily a detective was routinely photographing and investigating the death, when he suddenly noticed her chest rising and falling and said, 'She could have been in a body bag, by now,' how much luck can one have in this life?

*

Several years ago I was seriously ill lying in bed and, just after the doctor had visited, I went off into a deep sleep and began dreaming.

I dreamt that I was a little child and someone like Jesus picked me up and held me in his arms. He lifted me up inside a church or cathedral with beautifully carved wooden beams and many other woodcarvings. There were beautifully coloured windows, and the highest point of the roof formed like a tower and there was an opening through which shone a bright light. There in my dream I could see the blue sky with some tiny white clouds like angels floating around and the face of God in the centre looking down at me.

After waking up sweating I called my wife, telling her all about the dream, which felt as though I had come back from the dead. A few days later I got better and went back to work.

I also had a near death experience when I was shot through both legs in the last Great War, after falling over near a large tree, which I hoped would protect me, but did not. I lay on the ground in agony bleeding heavily, not being able to move, with other severely injured and dead soldiers around me for quite some time. Shooting began to start again and several more shots came my way injuring vital parts better not mentioned.

Agony took over once again and not being able to move, without being shot at again I had to lie there biting my teeth.

Suddenly a massive tank came rolling along towards my head and I was certain it would run right over me, but once again I was saved by millimetres.

The worst incident however – apart from jumping out of planes as a paratrooper in the war – seemed to be some years later when flying to South Africa with many others in a Jumbo-jet through a violent night-storm. The sky was lit up a fiery red colour with flashes of lightning, while the massive plane hopped about like a kangaroo, and continually fell from one air pocket to another. Everyone was scared stiff, and it seemed obvious that something was going to happen in mid-air, and sure enough it did.

One of the air-conditioning tanks burst its seams and water poured from the ceiling of the aircraft and sprayed everywhere. The air-crew and us passengers – some soaking wet – were unaware of what had happened at this split second, with the plane swinging from side to side and many screaming while trying to get out of their seats with air-crew running around. But all was sorted out once the details were known and all of us landed safely after one of the most frightening flights, although it did not stop us making several more.

⋆

Agonising illusions can bring fear to anyone, but one should always try to keep one's head up high and enjoy, if at all possible, the lovely sunshine high above.

Mentally transmitted sightings or illusions do and can happen to anyone anywhere and at any time.

Going back a few years, we stayed in a hotel in Portugal and when going to the bathroom I could quite distinctly see – having recognised from the television, but not having met personally – the image of Archbishop Tutu of South Africa with his red cap, vestment and face in the wall tiles and took a photo. I forwarded this out to him later with a letter describing the place and hotel.

Similarly, I was once staying with my wife in a hotel in Engtal, Austria – a very small place with just a farm and hotel right in the middle of the mountains at the very end of a pass. I was looking out of the window one time, after a day of brilliant sunshine followed by rain which later turned to light snow, when I noticed an image in the snow on one of the peaks. There I noticed a naturally etched and exact image of the head and chest of Nelson Mandela with a lion and an Alsatian lying on either side, guarding him. This I pointed out to my wife, who recognised the same image; he was at that time still president of South Africa.

Once again I was able to take a fairly good picture of this mountaintop, of which there were many all round us, outlining him and the two animals. I forwarded it to the President, with a letter and the address of the place, just in case he wanted to see himself in a naturally formed rock-face.

Images, or for that matter mentally transmitted pictures can often be seen by many people. In one newspaper back in January 1998, for example, showed a picture with the headline, 'I saw the face of Jesus in my duster,' from a lady. This I kept and still have it hanging on my wall, near the image of my late mother and others.

We had a carpet-runner in our bathroom at one time, and I would sit there quietly dreaming and see the image of my late mum, among other friends.

When my wife decided that we needed a new carpet-runner, I managed to preserve this piece and framed it, although previous to this I had already taken some photos to send away and keep.

⋆

We all live in a strange and yet perfect world, if only we were allowed to live in peace, with everyone recognising each other's faults or wisdoms.

The dear elderly Queen Mother before her departure from life often commented on what a wonderful world we live in, and when handed or given a present she would always say 'thank you', and that is what she always wanted, even if she had several of whatever it was. What a kind lady she was.

There are, no doubt, many people in this country, and around the world, who remember and will never forget this great lady, the Queen Mother, bless her.

And there are many good people around the world and again in this country who will never forget another lady, Princess Diana.

Chapter Eleven
(Experiences, Good or Bad)

Princess Diana had had very good as well as no doubt bad experiences in her young life, with some of them at times disturbing her mind or thoughts, but she was always able to open her heart to others she thought she could trust, particularly those friends close to her.

It appears now that she was not quite so lucky, and everything she divulged in secret seems now several years after her death, to be stirred up by her so-called friends and servants just for the sake of greed and making money.

Expressions can so easily be blown out of all proportion. How often have we heard different phrases or expressions in the course of the day or year, such as, 'If you do that again I will kill you,' but these are rarely meant seriously, or to cause any actual bodily harm. We are all humans using different expressions at times, which are not always the wisest, and others may misunderstand the meaning and thus sometimes mistakes or offences occur or are created, without any real intentions.

Diana may well have spoken or even written of such possibilities and giving the date or number '13' as an indication of fear, but she herself probably never thought a great deal about either nor felt any great concern.

She continued travelling and enjoying herself as she had always done. If only she had been left alone as she surely wanted at times, without any of the outside world's interference or jealousy by certain people.

As can now be seen and read, she must have been under constant pressure from many sides, when in the end she wanted to be free from continual attention. However photographers and many others, who seemingly knew exactly when and where she was at all times, kept in regular contact and pursuit of her every movement.

Is it possible that Diana did not wear a seat belt so she could hide her face and privacy from the many photographers who followed the car, just to get a picture of her for the media and spread her happiness around the world? Or maybe like myself, she was afraid that in the event of an accident and the car catching fire, she would not be able to release the seat belt, and no one else would be prepared to stick their head in the car to release it for fear of getting burnt and risking their own life.

It must have been an absolute nightmare, to be known so well and recognised by almost everyone, hoping to live a life in peace and tranquillity, especially when being young, attractive and seemingly in love again for the second time.

Yes it is almost certain that most people would have loved to see her happy smiling face again. Especially as it seemed she was enjoying life and was possibly in love again after two or more years of unhappiness and frustration.

It is very doubtful that anyone could really understand unless they had been in similar situations or circumstances themselves.

We, or most of us, are just human at the end of the day, and try our very best most times, which does not always work out just the way we expect or want it to. That is why it is most important to co-operate and jointly create happiness – not try to destroy it. That is the time when we all need a guiding hand, may this be from within, from ones elders, nature or maybe God himself; the belief in him has shown the way to many people lost in frustration.

We are all creatures on this earth and just like nature itself, we often need advice as to how to live our lives in peace, quite and tranquillity, which we all can do by just listening, and helping, rather than hindering others.

We are really no different to any animal, bird or other wildlife or plant; everything needs its freedom to strike roots, grow and hopefully live with respect to the natural age before dying.

I for one have always believed and trusted in my mum looking after me from high above after she passed away, God bless her. I lost her and her love in my early childhood, when she was taken from us after several years of operations after suffering from stomach cancer at a young age. None of us can ever predict as to how long we may enjoy this wonderful world. Like nature, some of us have to make room for others to survive.

*

Every year is slightly different; the year 2003 appears to have had its share of upheaval, starting from the war in Iraq, which went ahead without United Nations approval.

This war may have been won, but the fighting and upheavals still continue and will do so for many years to come, which will be detailed in my book *The Might of Terror*, written over the last two years but not yet completed.

However, some good nearly always comes out of any upheaval. Queen Elizabeth II's 50th or Golden Anniversary to the throne was held under glorious weather for almost its entirety. 2003 was one of the finest sunniest and dry years we have had for a long time, with most apart from farmers enjoying themselves. The same year Concord, one of the finest and fastest Aeroplanes ever built, was cheered on by the crowds as it made its final flight after 20 years and has now been grounded forever. Around the same time the aforementioned book about Princess Diana appeared and stirred up people's memories in this country and elsewhere to a point of despair.

At the time of writing this the President of the United States, George Bush, has decided to come to Britain with massive guards for protection at the cost of many million pounds[29], to try and make peace with many members of this country with a smile, after pulling the British people into a war of no return.

There are people who believed they were right to start this aggressive war, but there are many in Britain and around the world, who thought it wrong but had no choice but to follow, while many innocent people were and still are being killed on all sides. One newspaper's headline and picture, 'Howdy partner, great to see y'all' showed President Bush with a broad smile pointing into the dark and Prince Charles his usual self walking beside him, appearing to not give a damn.

If this President George Bush is such a great and admired person, fighting for freedom, why does he have to enclose himself with millions of pounds worth of protective bullet-proof cars and massive body guards, what is he afraid of?

Perhaps he knows, or it appears, that 'The Might of Terror' has suddenly become very much greater than the most powerful nation in the world.

This aggressive war in Iraq, and the Middle East, was given no backing by the United Nations, thus undermining it, which is a shameful situation.

Some of the national newspapers, such as the *Daily Mirror*, appear to have been against this war of aggression, leaving President George Bush and our Prime Minister Tony Blair very much going it alone from the beginning.

These papers appear to have scored points rather well, by breaking this so-called sound security system or ring, which no concrete blocks or walls will keep out of the great house of Westminster or any other.

Just give the old 'Iron Curtain' and concrete wall in Berlin after World War II a thought, or is this too long ago, for young Ministers to remember?

Massive concrete towers, walls or blocks and many other protections have been used over a long period of time, but there will always be those that find their way in by going around or over, and will penetrate it in due course.

*

As the old saying goes, 'One can try and kill off some ants, rats or mice, but there will always be some which survive to breed again.'

Chapter Twelve
(Relationships and Agonies)

It seems wise that, whatever the name of any national-paper, they should have a mixture of opinions that not only support one point of view, especially when there are so many people willing to walk the streets in opposition to this aforementioned war. It most certainly looks or appears like that. You would think that propaganda within the national papers has almost certainly been financially assisted, but to prove so is another matter and would be very difficult and costly.

If Bush is as powerful as is continually proclaimed, why is there often so much fear showing in the face of our so-called 'British friend'?

One begins to wonder if this friendship is as deep as it is so often portrayed or whether this visit arranged at this particular time was just to show how strong the relationship between Britain and America really is?

This relationship, however, shows that it is not as strong as it was made out to be and seems somewhat in doubt, especially since President Bush of the United States appears slightly concerned about the possibility of NATO being dismantled, and he is once again trying to show his power.

Ken Livingston the Mayor of London an outspoken person appears to have made a so-called outrageous attack on George Bush. When he said, shortly before holding a 'peace party' at City Hall in London, 'I don't formally recognize George Bush because he was not officially elected. So we are organizing an alternative reception for everybody who is not George Bush,'[30] he was clearly going to be criticised by many of the national papers, even if he was correct.

There is however that old saying, 'Freedom of press, and freedom of speech,' the first part some papers appear to love, but not the second unless it is in their own interest and favour.

If someone like President George Bush or our own Tony Blair continually pronounced they would never go to war without a just cause, and then do the exact opposite, who can people believe?

As many times it has been said and written in the past, and no doubt the future too, problems between countries should be sorted out by negotiations, without firing a shot if at all possible, just like within an ordinary family. If this is expected from ordinary people with laws having been introduced for this purpose, then surely the Governments and leaders of such should have the decency to follow them too.

It may at times be very difficult to find someone who can negotiate between two stubborn heads at the very top, and for this reason the United Nations Security Council was established and should be allowed to do their job.

This authority, to which most nations belong, should never have been sidestepped by any so-called powerful nation. If there are persons who are prepared to override all laws, they should not be surprised to hear outspoken words, or find thousands of protesters on the streets outside places such as Buckingham Palace.

One cartoon portrayed the Duke of Edinburgh with double barrel shotgun and cartridges lying on the wall, looking out of a skylight of the palace, with the Queen in the background. The Duke is asking the surrounding protection forces, 'You seem a bit short up here, I wondered if you need any help?' This cartoon seemed rather amusing, especially after the Duke had chosen to walk behind the President, who was inspecting the guards of the Palace without fear of being shot at by terrorists. I couldn't help noticing when I saw this spectacle, that, with the usual grin on his face, there seemed absolutely no fear in the Duke who appeared quite relaxed as he followed President Bush.

President George Bush is said to have told the bereaved British families that the soldiers 'did not die in vain'[31], but he forgot to say; 'They most likely suffered a great deal of agony and pain.'

Is it not strange that some people never appear to think about the agonies and pain (even if not wounded or killed) that some soldiers have to go through on their leader's behalf, just to satisfy the greed they have set themselves? Why should it always be the young and innocent who have to carry out their master's request in turmoil and agony? Especially when in the very end these masters just walk away with most of the recognition and maybe even a statue.

What about many of those who may have survived but have to carry certain agonies and pain for the rest of their lives, with no one giving a damn. One cannot help but think that the only people benefiting is their president and our own prime minister, who will no doubt be strengthening their relationship, thus aiding trade between the two countries.

And what about the many who have to go on suffering for many years thereafter, with little or no compensation?

Have any of you, by any chance heard about 'The Little Bush and the Large Oak Tree'? It seems that one fell over upon the other and squashed it, but not having been there, I am not sure which fell upon which, maybe we'll find out one day.

Which got squashed is hard to tell,
It depends, how quick the Oak Tree fell.
The Little Bush has run away,
But will it start again, one day?

It seems that one of the previous Presidents of America, Ronald Reagan, had one special and specific expression, 'You ain't seen nothing yet!' which might well be true if one lives long enough to find out or see. It is always said that time is a great healer to anyone given that time, but many, are not quite that fortunate.

Protesters against the visit of President George Bush and the war in Iraq have turned out by the thousands blocking and marching through the streets of London and toppling an effigy of the President at Trafalgar Square, to the delight of many, and to the anger of others.

These marches through London, New York and many other places so far appear to have gone reasonably well and peaceful, without great disturbance caused; only surprised looks on the faces of our prime minister and the US president. However, our Prime Minister was to remark, looking rather stern faced, that we should remember that such demonstrations could not have been held in Baghdad under Sadaam Hussein, but seemingly very similar more forceful demonstrations are presently being held there by many, who do not appear to be as happy as thought with this war or occupation. Perhaps there was no need to hold any demonstrations in that country on previous occasions?

We are supposed to live in a free society and thus those people who wish to stand up for themselves, should surely have the right to do so and be listened to without being denied their liberty.

It was claimed and reported that in a telephone survey there were forty per cent against and sixty per cent for this Presidential visit and war in Iraq, which seemed quite a high proportion on either side. But what about those who did not bother to phone?

What ever the percentages might be, everyone in a democracy surely has a right for their point of view to be considered and listened to, not just ignored like rotten apples on the ground.

Terror is not in every human being. Terror is and has always been created by depression and unnecessary force being used, which will most likely turn into a 'Might of Terror' It might even go underground, and come up unforeseen and completely unexpected, without it showing all its force beforehand (as appears to have been shown, before this last aggressive war).

It seems such a waste of human life and bringing misery when every man has once again to fight for him or herself just to survive.

Most people, including myself, do not agree with 'Terror' but one must think first; how, why and who created the terror, mentioned and why did it come about? And how can it be controlled? Forcing a dog to go wild, shooting it and allowing many others to get hurt in the process, maybe just through seeing and experiencing it, is certainly not the way, and will encourage others to turn into wild dogs.

There are so many problems like poverty, misery, unemployment, killing and destruction, mostly brought about by governments or leaders, which can only lead to terror. Similar to wasting peoples hard earned cash through taxes by rushing into a war and have vast expenditures thrown away on state visits and conferences without bringing results; and all this created by leaders who should know better. Only determination, patience with humans, negotiations or even neighbourly love will allow others to see your points of view. Democracy presently appears to be rotting away instead of being put into practice at this present time.

If Britain and especially America used democracy as it should be, they would see it is such a fine thing, with freedom for all. Why have the United States so far not managed to persuade neighbouring countries like Mexico, Panama, Cuba, Colombia and many others further south to take it up and follow suit?

President Bush has been saying, 'There's a debate going on as to whether people like the Iraqis will ever adapt to the habits of freedom. There's an elitism that feels they can't adapt the habits of democracy,'[32] but he strongly disagrees.

It seems somewhat immoral to welcome a man into Britain whom many of us disagree with his policies. It is as though we are saying 'We have all the money to spare to allow you George and Laura Bush to stand with our Royal Family and all our VIPs at a ceremonial welcome protected by horses and Palace guards.' Followed by, 'We are happy for you and the first lady to join all of us at a banquet at Buckingham Palace with the Queen, Prince Phillip and most of our ministers, with speeches on how to run down the rest of the world who do not agree with us, like Europe.'

But what will happen if and when all these defences are broken down and no longer available?

It was thought that our Prime Minister Tony Blair looked rather drawn and thin, as if he could do with a good three-course dinner followed by wine or Diet Coke! Especially since his pretty wife Cherie Blair seemingly blasted the Bush Administration in regards to their campaign against the International Criminal Court, which you would think was not too well received by husband Tony Blair. In this respect however the lady is right, why should the powerful United States continually refuse, the way to better the world, as with Global warming?

President George Bush like many before him appears to have an attitude of we can stand on our own feet, and we shall determine what is good and what is bad in this world, never mind the rest. While this president of the USA was well protected while visiting Britain, the terrorist group Al-Qaeda struck in Turkey, killing more people in revenge and so it will go on.

Will our leaders ever come to their senses and start talking rather than spending billions on visits and banquets, which are of no use to any one, but continually worsen the situation?

At that time they even pronounced that they would not give an inch, we will stand firm, a phrase that has been used so many times in the past and no doubt will be use by the other side.

Every one prefers, 'To take the extra mile or a country,' which must be stopped before it is too late.

A similar, but luckily bomb-free, uprising or as called, 'A Velvet Revolution' has begun in Georgia, another close

American ally with the war in Iraq. The President Eduard Shevardnadze, a previous foreign minister of Russia or former USSR and great friend of former US President George Bush senior, appears to have lost control after eleven years, and is alleged to have fixed the last election.[33]

No country having supported the USA and UK in the aggressive war against Iraq appears to look that favourable, even in America itself uprisings against President Bush seem to be taking place.

This discontentment has been followed by more and more enquiries, as to who was right, or wrong and what information was followed and why. Money appears to be no object when it comes to showing how the two leaders were not at fault for starting such a war. But it will no doubt be seen as a white wash by the public before they even begin to investigate.

Caution may have been the best in the very first place, but it is never too late for any army to retreat, however hard it might feel, oil or land is nowhere as important as self-respect or life itself.

A nuclear holocaust has already been forecast around 2006, which is just around the corner, when no two million pound armoured 'Cadillac De Ville' or a vast amount of bodyguards will be any use for protection.

At least this time the powerful president of the United States has made it back home safe again and will no doubt thank Tony Blair for his smiles and assistance, but most certainly not many of the British people or protesters.

One old saying goes, 'Most countries are like fruit, the worms are always inside', which may well be considered, or 'Fear is the mother of morality' and 'Morality is the best of all devices for leading mankind by the nose'. All of these are of great importance, and all should be remembered, as they may well turn out to be true. These phrases have no doubt been written down by people, who have in their past experienced all the upheavals we are seemingly following, without the appreciation of their quality.

Chapter Thirteen
(Suspicions and Truth)

It often amazes me that someone has persuaded many of the people in this world to believe that men have actually landed on the Moon, even-though it is reported to be impossible to penetrate and go through the thick layer of radiation activity in the outer atmosphere[34], without the destruction of human life at this present moment in time.

They are now already talking about sending men to Mars, after satellites with robots are said to have successfully landed and taken pictures, which is still debatable. It seems mice have been chosen to be used first, to see if they could possibly survive, which is quite a clever idea, but one cannot help but feel sorry for the poor mice.

The more that the destruction of the two towers on September 11th 2001 is mentioned or preached about by the President of the United States, the more speculation and conspiracy theories abound that the US Government or destructive Agencies could have been involved. If this was true, what a way to create hatred within ones own people against another country or countries? Terrorism is nasty and similar to war, with many innocent people getting killed unnecessarily, but when this is and has been created by high-powered capitalism for their own gain, that is even worse, and virtually undetectable.

All this might seem crazy, but just think of the persons, who continually keep saying, 'Honestly it was not my fault, honestly,' is he believed in the long run? Most people would naturally think this to be very unlikely or even silly, but allow us to think of the last few years, when the US have been desperate to create a safety net or shield to keep out possible long-range nuclear missiles. Apparently, they even tried to involve Britain and the European continent to intercept such missiles, in other words, allow all the shit fall upon anyone, but not on the USA.

What does one have to do, to first guide a shotgun to hit a target? One has to build or create a target to aim and aim at it again and again. Fast moving targets are not the easiest and much too expensive to continually build or create.

Thus a standing target to be attacked by one moving would be a great deal easier in the beginning to try and get the magnetic, electronic wave direction and pulling power for destruction correct and perfect.

Newly built and heavily insured buildings with every important document copied and stored away would be ideal. The building and equipment can easily be replaced from the massive insurance money; especially if it has been done with most people's belief by someone who seemingly cannot be found or traced.

Airliners, of which there are many and all belonging to different private or national companies, can again be separately insured, and life it seems is of little importance.

Old buildings would be much too suspicious and of little value in regard to the years of outlay and little return. Guidance systems can easily be built into any building or airliner without a great deal of suspicion or any one knowing.

The scandals surrounding the large multi-billion, national company Enron, have led to people connecting it with September 11th too.

Some people might say these must have been suspicious minds, but surely when lives are lost, should not everything or everyone be investigated and questioned?

It also seems strange, that the USA very soon after managed to shoot down one of their own guided missiles over the oceans, or has this been forgotten?

Not that it is intended to lay any suspicions against anyone without foundation; all possibilities must and could be assumed, similar to weapons of mass destruction have been.

One question has recently been asked in the papers, 'What do we know about Laura Bush, America's First Lady?' But I would like to ask, 'What exactly do we really know about President George Bush?' whose election incidentally appears to have been largely financed by such multi million companies like Enron.

There seem to be many questions, still to be asked and answered in all cases, before we arrive at the truth and nothing but the truth, can surely be acceptable.

Large headlines appeared in our national papers, 'Operation Big Bang; Tough new laws to protect us from terrorism.'[35] Are we all now beginning to fear this we have ourselves created, but not yet learned to control?

Our leaders in our so-called Democracy appear to spread nothing but dictatorial ideas, especially again lately when it seems that they wish to force asylum seekers out and even propose to take away their children.

Methods of this sort do not bring about the best relations between people, and creating more and more resentment and terrorism.

Is it not about time that humanitarian assistance takes priority, rather than hate creating methods?

If certain people could only hear themselves talk or maybe think, everywhere you look there is nothing but uprisings and bad feelings, even with the Middle Eastern problem of Israel and Palestine; as well as Afghanistan, Iraq, recently Turkey and now Georgia.

All of these start from small beginnings, very similar to the subject this book is all about, and should be seriously looked into and carefully considered.

Are these agonising problems really worth taking? When some person's greed, hate or jealousy; results in another's miserable painful death, with following agonies for many others.

Chapter Fourteen
(Closeness and Understanding)

One might ask, 'What has all this to do with Princess Diana, her peaceful and happy life, full of love and kindness, followed by upheaval and later tragic fatal accident, all so completely unnecessary?'

Looking at it in detail, quite a lot. We are all trying to live a life of happiness and coping with despair as it comes. Often the end comes too early and unexpected, when many times this could easily be avoided or prevented, if only some would try to look, listen and begin to understand.

Yes, the late Princess Diana was most certainly a happy go lucky lady showing a completely different outlook to life, whereas her at that time sister-in-law Princess Anne, or better said Princess Royal, who similarly is a fine lady, adopts a somewhat different outlook to life, most likely due to her royal up-bringing.

Our Princess Royal is very much more refined in her way of meeting and talking to people. She is more like her brother Prince Charles – although full of smiles, most of the time, there appears to be that slight distance between Royalty and the person in the street.

This may not be a bad thing at times, but the ordinary people in the street require that little belonging and closeness as was shown by the late Queen Mother and has been in some way more than transferred to Queen Elizabeth II.

Everyone, or at least most people, appreciate this and are looking for and want to touch, which naturally is not always possible or the very best, but allows that warm feeling.

Princess Diana had and spread that feeling of belonging, openness and love to most people she met, without any restraint. Now Prince William appears to follow in his mother's footsteps, with his soft, restrained, sincere and gracious smile, while Prince Harry is following the more open outgoing laughter and happiness of his mother.

We all know that a great sincere smile can often be followed with a background of harshness, and no doubt Princess Diana possessed both, but naturally showed the best side of her face and body to the public and that is what is by most people required, and looked forward to.

All of us should be more open minded trying to show the best, not the worst side of ourselves to friends and neighbours, even other countries and their leaders need to understand that we cannot all be the same. But we all have the same feelings, when it comes to illnesses, injuries or even hardship, and the more we try to understand, the easier it will be to live together in harmony and understanding.

Talking and negotiating with others in a peaceful manner is the only way we shall manage to live in peace. Trying to be powerful and showing ones muscles by hitting others not so strong for the purpose of showing off or for a few coppers is senseless, and should be unacceptable.

This herein mentioned understanding, and loving thy neighbour, colour or religion should however begin at the very top of society and leaderships, not only expected from others lower down. It certainly is preached enough, just like freedom, but who will understand it and most important when?

It seems that at the time of writing this book, Sophie, the Countess of Wessex and the wife of Prince Edward the younger son of our Queen, is catching the headlines quite frequently.

She with her happy seemingly sincere smile, looks very similar to Princess Diana, and has had the great fortune of giving birth to a beautiful girl, whom as Sophie said, '...is wonderful.'[36]

Both Edward and Sophie seemed delighted once Sophie was allowed to leave hospital and return home, while the small premature born baby was retained for a little while longer and then eventually allowed to join her parents.

The Queen and Prince Phillip, the grandparents, could clearly not wait and apparently paid a secret visit to see their newly born granddaughter, obviously desperate to see the new addition to the Royal family.

The baby when born, weighed just 4lb 9oz. On leaving the hospital, the countess said, 'I cannot thank the staff and medical team and nurses at Frimley Park enough for all they have done for me and our beautiful daughter who will be joining us at home to complete our family very soon.'[37]

No name had at that time been chosen for the baby daughter, and Sophie was handed a bouquet of flowers from the nursing staff as she left hospital with her husband Edward pushing her in a wheelchair to the main entrance.

A new member was added to the Royal Family shining a bright light over all of them in that difficult time just before Christmas 2003, which must have been a wonderful feeling and much appreciated.

I am sure most of the country, and certainly my family and I, would like to forward the best of wishes to all, especially since Sophie and Edward had such bad luck with her first pregnancy.

Chapter Fifteen
(Enjoy Life and Smile)

Coming back to the late Princess Diana, it is reported that around twenty videos in which she is said to discuss intimate details of her relationship with Prince Charles are now under investigation by the courts in regard to ownership.[38]

The police had seemingly found these videotapes in Paul Burrell's possession, which appear to have been confiscated and kept in Scotland Yard's safe keeping until the court decides ownership.

Hopefully it will be decided to hand these tapes back to her family, rather than an outsider; however close he or she thought they were to the Princess. No doubt a great deal more muck could be spread, when in the end it might reach the good lady's nose, which should be avoided if at all possible.

Similarly, the Queen was seen to smile broadly, when asked recently to unveil, in many peoples opinion, the seemingly rudest statue in Britain.[39]

Chuckles appeared to have broken out among the crowd, with the Duke of Edinburgh shading his eyes, but the Queen appeared unperturbed. She in fact later played football with a four-year old boy in the street, no doubt to take her mind off this statue.

Princess Diana however would have been proud of her younger son Prince Harry, who was at that particular time staying in Australia. He took it upon himself, in the spirit of a teenager, to get down onto the field congratulating and embracing the English rugby team players for winning the world cup in Australia for the fist time in almost forty years. This no doubt his mum would have enjoyed as much as he did.

Prince Harry like all the other British supporters in the crowd was full of cheers, laughing and shouting, waving hands and hats and completely overwhelmed. As I imagine were all the supporters at home in clubs, pubs or in their own home in front of the TV, it was most certainly a great sight to see in so many years. No doubt his elder brother Prince William and his dad Charles the Prince of Wales, with the rest of the Royal Family, were also delighted. The Queen is in fact reported to have forwarded her sincere thanks and congratulations to the team, at that time still out in Australia, saying, 'Victory will never be so sweet again'.

The team has now returned with the gold cup to massive cheers and jubilation from the British crowds with great smiles on their faces. That is something people need and want most everyday, to retain happiness, not accusations and sorry stories to make everyone sad and miserable. We are all one people and a good laugh or smile does a lot more good to all and everyone. Never forget the phrase, 'Just smile a while and while you smile another smile appears', which is surely better than many eyes full of tears.

That was our Princess Diana, always full of smiles for everyone, even when lending a helping hand, lifting the long white train of her friend's wedding dress down the stairs and watching her own footsteps at the same time.

Even as a young wife, when she showed herself in uniform as the colonel in chief in Northern Ireland, boosting the moral of the troops, she was full of smiles. And once again she was full of laughs and jokes about her clumsy heavy army boots, which made her feet look huge. But even in the baggy army jacket and baggy trousers she seemed to look stunning with her hair tidy in place and a smile on her face for all.

Princess Diana, once again full of smiles, but showing a little sadness, when she is reported to have told a soldier that she thought him mad to be getting married.

She had that wonderful ability to make people feel comfortable with her, wherever she went and whoever she met, hiding her own feelings.

It was not long after this that the news was flashed around the country, of her marriage with Prince Charles breaking up.

Princess Diana however carried on regardless, although one could see the sadness deep in her eyes and heart at times, she seemed resilient to gossip or sneering remarks in the media and produced a sincere smile whenever any camera snapped away.

Diana's genuine caring brought such a lot of comfort and joy to most people, especially to the young sick or injured children, but she never forgot many of the elderly and appeared to care for all and everyone.

One could obviously go on and on writing about this much photographed Princess, who no doubt had a wonderful time in the few years she had the pleasure to be with us and we have never forgotten the memories we had of her.

Princess Diana, no longer alive, and her smiles a distant past, one would have thought, we, or at the very least, most of us, should now allow her to rest in peace and quiet.

There has just recently once again been a write up about the French police and the enquiry they carried out, which seemingly was not as expected, or at least not for many people in this country.

Although every country has its own methods of procedure, a few comments to be remembered might be in order. Commander Mules of the French Police said, 'Secrets are secret, so we never could have pierced the secret.'[40]

It seems that the police chief seemed to be more concerned about the French doctors and medical professors, than what had happened to Princess Diana.

He said earlier with a reported shrug of the shoulder, 'There are fifteen traffic accidents like this every day in France.'[41] And he followed later by saying, 'Imagine that an autopsy is performed which later might discredit the great professors.'[42] Surely a great man such as this professor cannot be seen to make a mistake like any ordinary person?

Commander Mules, appears to have insisted, that a higher authority than himself had taken the decision, before the body was released. 'Even the top police inspectors of the crime squad do not know about these things that take place at a diplomatic level,' he said. Now more than four years after the French closed their files on Diana, virtually nothing would make the police reopen them Commander Mules is reported to have said, and added, 'There is no reason to do so. The verdict has been given and the case is closed.'[43]

This is slightly different from what was said earlier, but who can one believe or trust these days? Reopening old wounds will certainly do no one any good, unless it is for the sake of finding out and knowing the truth. This however, in the end might open new wounds, which may never heal or bring good news.

Some of us have to pass away earlier than expected, to make room for new generations, so that these have room to spread their roots or wings, like plants or trees in the soil, or birds in flight

It was such a great shame for this white rose of England, Princess Diana to have been taken from us at an early age, but at least she did not have to suffer for many years like many others have to do.

The Princess

Prince Charles,
The Prince of Wales,
Picked a Princess,
A rose of fairy tales.

She was so sweet,
The best of all,

But in the end allowed,
Petals to fall.

This Princess was not quite,
What royalty thought,
Although for years they smiled
And tears they fought.

The love was great;
They had two sons,
With most years full
Of laughs and fun.

It was only later
When the rot set in,
With the butler's
Jealousies and spin.

The marriage failed
And they split up,
The British people's
Worst hiccup.

They loved
This Princess of Wales,
With all her smiles
And funny tales.

She seemed to have
The time of life with all,
She was so pretty,
Slender and quite tall.

Until she had to part
From us and earth,
She certainly had
All that she was worth.

A person, people and children,
Never forget,
That she had to go so early,
We all do regret.

K-WA

Chapter Sixteen
(In Remembrance)

I hope that this proposed gushing memorial fountain and pond (in memory of Princess Diana), forecast to cost three million pounds, will be ready and working in Hyde Park, London, by the time this book is published.

No doubt the general public will be more than pleased to be able to take their children to see it and splash about as previously written about in one of my earlier books, 'The Golden Crown'.

This novel use of water, flowing and cascading or tumbling down through and over the rocks, is supposed to portray the Princess's gentleness and sense of humour, with the rocks representing some of the turmoil in her life.

The design comprising a large oval of flowing water, which can be touched by grown-ups and children alike, is to depict the brilliance of the Princess's glitter in sunshine or rain.

It is said that all the money to have this very well designed, proposed memorial built, will come out of the Princess memorial fund, to which many people have contributed over the past years, in memory of this fine upstanding person.

May she, rest in peace, but be allowed to look down from above and enjoy as she has always done upon the people and children below.

It is surely recognised, that not every one will have the same concerns or memory of Princess Diana, while others might have much deeper feelings, especially her two sons, William and Harry, who have now grown up. At the time of their mother's funeral they were still teenagers, walking upright like the rest of the Royal Family behind her with the white roses, tulips and lilies upon the covering of the Royal standard draped coffin, being carried into Westminster Abbey.

Even though the boys and royal family walking behind seemed restrained, and in no doubt deep sorrow, the people and children outside were in tears, to have lost such a great person so early in her life.

Although the author has had no real personal contact with Princess Diana, this book has been written, in the memory of her fine quality and remembrance of the great work, she has done for the community at large.

We all know that she did not have the time to finish, this, her fine work, which will surely continue in her absence. May she continue to fulfil her wishes in her afterlife, as she was able to do when she was with us, years in which we all enjoyed the fruits of her hard work and perseverance.

Bad thoughts and accusations will diminish in the years to come and people you have not been able to trust will decline.

May God, like most of us be with you and allow you the rest and peace many of us so dearly wish you to have, and you yourself are now looking for.

I am sure many others will continue your kind thoughts for humanity in your absence.

The Young Diana

The young and beautiful Diana always had a smile,
The time you were with us, was only a short while.

But no one will forget you, of this you can be sure,
For your serious accident, there seemed to be no cure.

The unsolved mysteries of your quick death,
Seem so far-fetched and such a mess.

There are people, very much concerned,
Much out of this must now be learned.

You were the glory of this land,
To every one a mighty friend.

You may no longer be with us,
But some do like to make a fuss.

Don't be disturbed, we'll think of you,
Whatever you did, or do,
Will not effect the friends you've had,
In your best times or now in bad.

We all hope, you'll have the best,
While you lay there, to have your rest.

This is the least you now deserve,
In this our lovely Universe.

To this beautiful and young Princess,
All we can say, 'May God, you bless.'

K-WA

Through the depth of dark clouds, there will nearly always blink a new and bright shining star, which sometimes takes a little while to see, but it has and with some luck, will continue forever, with you, Diana, having been left to keep it alight.

We all know this can be of no great comfort to you up there with all the other Angels, looking down upon all of us from high above, but no doubt you will be guided in the right direction

There has however a new brightly shining star been born upon this earth, a baby girl, of your brother and sister-in-law, Prince Edward and Sophie. Both parents seem to be over the moon with the girl's safe arrival.

Now after Sophie and her newly born girl had been separated for some time in hospital they are now, all three happy together again, in their own home, with all eyes sparkling.

The newly born has at long last been given the name of 'Lady Louise Windsor'; the full name is to be, Louise Alice Elizabeth Mary Mountbatten-Windsor.

This may be quite a mouthful, but seems to take most of the more famous names, from Edward's great-great-grandmother, Louise of Hesse-Cassel, his paternal grandmother Princess Alice of Greece, his grandmother, Elizabeth 'Queen Mum', as well as the royal mother-in-law, Sophie's smiling mother, Mary Rhys-Jones.

The couple specially chose four traditional regal names for the latest addition to the Royal Family, although she will not have the HRH title, but is and no doubt will be the sparkle of everyone's eyes, although doubtfully overtaking Diana. The idea it seems was to distance their blue-eyed little daughter, who was allowed to go home to Bagshot Park, Surrey, from future royal duties

She has already been shown to the people, in the national papers, and appears to have a smile similar to Diana's.

All names are well connected with Prince Edward, his wife Sophie and the Royal family, from Queen Elizabeth II and Prince Phillip the Duke of Edinburgh's side of the family. It seems that Princess Anne, the Princess Royal, already shares three of the names, Alice, Louise and Elizabeth. Prince Edward and his wife Sophie first sought the Queen's approval before naming the three-week-old Lady Louise Windsor.

The couple, Prince Edward and Sophie, have been shown beaming in delight, holding the well wrapped up little girl in Edwards arms, with Sophie close by.

May this be a lasting happiness, which we are all certain you Princess Diana would wish as much as we all do.

The delay of nearly three weeks came about because the couple wanted to leave out the name Mountbatten-Windsor, and just call the little girl Wessex, after the Prince Edward and wife Sophie of Wessex, but it was thought right to be included.

It is however great to know that the original Duke of Edinburgh's Princess Alice of Greece, as well as his great grandmother Princess Louise was included, to keep the early tradition of the Royal Families intact. Although there have been some venomous views printed in at least one of the recent newspapers, whose points of view I have considered deeply. The Author (myself) not being of the same opinion, (although not entirely royal in his out-look) one should sympathise to a certain extent; after all what has a name or the length of it to do with any obsession?

It has been written that the royal family should adopt smaller names and should be much smaller in size, since the public simply won't wear large numbers of royals with long names, who are subsidised one way or another by the taxpayers. This, one would have thought, seems a great deal of nonsense that people get into their heads at times.

The Royal Family surely bring far more money into the Chancellor of the Exchequers purse (especially from other countries) than many of the ordinary families who are continually subsidised by the state.

Whether their name originally came from Saxe-Coburg-Gotha, Germany or in the case of Prince Phillip arising from Schleswig-Holstein-Sonderburg-Glucksburg as suggested, by the writer Mark Bolland[44] seems quite irrelevant to most people in this country.

All of us are somehow related back some thousands of years and still do not know exactly where we originated from and no doubt all have venom in our blood. Most no doubt are delighted that the above named has certain traditional views on some of the previous Royals herein written about, and the person mentioned will attend The National Aids Trust, as he so kindly referred to.

This, being one of Diana's charities, which indeed would have reminded all of them or us, of the danger. Her charities no doubt, like most of us miss her badly.

Chapter Seventeen
(Photographic Publicity)

While Prince Harry, the younger son of Princess Diana, appeared to enjoy himself playing cowboys and Indians in some cattle range in Australia, everyone at home seems to be enjoying the newly born. It surely will not be long before the Press will manage to get the first real pictures of this little girl for all to see and admire.

Prince Edward and Sophie might not be too keen for the little beauty to be spread all over the newspapers, the public would no doubt like to see her with her mother or parents, in due course.

Although we have all seen the baby in the arms of the Edward and Sophie, most would wish to see the little girl walking and playing about with her parents at some later time. It must at times be very hard to live with; being before the cameras and in the public eye day after day, which many people would not appreciate.

Although many of the film stars and pretty girls might like it, it is doubtful that many of the Royal Family appreciate the continual clicking of cameras on every occasion. The public might appreciate decent pictures, but is there any need for hundreds of cameramen following and being snap-happy?

Surely some of these snap-happy people would not be too happy if cameras were to follow them everywhere they went? It seems this was certainly a concern of Princess Diana on many occasions. Although one can be certain that there were certain occasions the Princess appreciated photos taken of her in public and on her many walkabout's. On other occasions though, when she was pursued with long distance cameras on holidays, we can be certain she would have preferred to have been kept out of the spotlight.

Nothing surely can be more aggravating than having to look over one's shoulder ever second of the day as to who, where or when someone is trying to take a snap, when one least expects it. Surely not every one wishes to end up on page three of certain newspapers, even if they have a perfect body. There are certainly many, who wish to keep their privacy only for the nearest and dearest to see and admire.

Although a nice looking and well shaped body, will always be admired by most, not everyone is happy and willing to show all to the general public. Then there are also those who are not as nice as they think they are, but why turn down ready cash? But one can be sure, born or married into the Royal family, that Royals would never consider taking such handouts, their publicity is for free.

Your Boys

Your two boys were born to be Royal,
And those, to you, are more than loyal.

Although some people are just jealous,
And others being very callous.

Don't take these, too much to heart,
Most would just love to take some part.

Do not let them; spoil your ever-lasting rest,
While you were here you've done your best.

Allow your boys to have their fun,
Like Harry as a cowboy, on some horses run.

Prince William smiles and tries to laugh,
While young Harry, seems to be quite tough.

They are like you Dian' in many ways,
And presently have some bad days.

Protecting you, the best they can,
But do not know, quite how and when.

You are not here to guide their way,
They, like you, have got to take it day by day.

Do not concern yourself, but have your rest,
You can be sure; they'll try, like you, their very best.

K-WA

In fact most of us do and so do your charities, and people, who have been chosen to carry on, your good work started, although there seems some little doubt about these mentioned, lately. It looks in fact that even these your charities appear to have somewhat overspent, in the last few years, like almost everyone.

It has recently been written and no doubt most would agree, as I do, that the recently born Lady Louise Wessex, would or could have been the final stage of a great tradition of the royal re-branding. Is it really the Royal Family, which needs re-branding, or is it the Government, and in some cases the public?

Be it how much the Royal Family cost or how much is spent on them, I am sure they do not demand this, but are being paid or allowed, from the Chancellor of the Exchequer, out of public funds.

Surely this can easily be controlled as to how much the country, can afford?

It could be said that the Royal Family contributes a great deal to the Exchequer from their agricultural and other income, for which they surely have to pay taxes, just like anyone else?

I would have thought that these expenditures continually referred to could surely be controlled, say as to how much can be made available or in accordance to how much these visits are considered worthy of bringing in trade and other friendly connections to the country.

Similar to the colour of guards provided for their protection, which has recently been mentioned. The Royal Family does not appear to have a say in this matter, and neither, one can be certain, would they wish to have.

It has always been many people's opinion including mine, that all Royals have been as happy to shake hands with whoever they meet, whatever colour, on their many tours.

Similarly it has been great to read that the first black police bodyguard, Sergeant Les Turner, who will accompany royal members and other VIPs on official and foreign tours, has asked not to be given special privileges or favours. In other words he does not want to make an issue of his colour and just wants to get on with his job, and appears to be a valuable addition to the squad.

The sergeant seemingly made his first public appearance, when he guarded the Countess of Wessex, while she was in hospital having her baby.

This brings us back to the previous controversial issue and choice of name for the new addition to the Royal Family. It would surely be better if jealous persons could try at all times considered other people's feelings and choices, which do not hurt anyone.

Everyone, or at least most, have been proud of their names for centuries, which in many cases are a sort of heritage, like a ring, photo or whatever one might treasure.

There are obviously people who do not like their names, for reasons to be respected. Tradition, however, from the Author's point of view should be of vital importance to each and everyone, whether this be a name, dialect or song and which in the end may well die like all of us will at some time or other. Names, like treasures, should be avoided being lost forever.

Treasures

Treasure thy name and treasure thy offspring's,
More than treasure most other things.

These are the one's, which continue to live,
And in the end they are more likely prepared to give.

People often take what does not belong,
And don't give a hoot or even a song.

If you do not treasure, what you have been given,
You might in the end not be forgiven.

Is what we treasure, really a treasure,
Not necessarily gold, diamonds or just leisure.

Respect what we have been left from past generations,
And never stop any thought of new creations.

We all treasure to see different lands and their shapes,
From very small, wild animals right up to the apes.

The latter may well be the race, from which we were created,
So try to love every one else and you'll not be hated.

Allow us to leave what we ourselves have created,
For others to treasure and later be dated.

Like our forefather's have done in the past,
And most things done well will forever last.

K-WA

Chapter Eighteen
(New Enquiries)

It seems that Mr Fayed, the over seventy-year-old father of Dodi, and many other people were or are not satisfied with the lack of a public inquiry in England into the death of Princess Diana. Since the English courts were not prepared to have a proper inquiry into the fatal accident, Mr Fayed has chosen to take the matter to a Scottish court in Edinburgh.

Although the Scottish court has now allowed such inquiry to go ahead in the hope of finding out the facts of this accident, Royal watchers welcomed the announcement of an inquest and public hearing on British soil in January, which was subsequently adjourned.

It seems that the Royal Family is once more allowing the right of proceedings, which is better late, than never.

Although it is very difficult to believe in some theories or conspiracies, some hearings in this country are absolutely vital and necessary to clear up misunderstandings and satisfy the public in general.

Even if it is going to be just a formality, especially since slanderous accusations have been brought about, which should and must be cleared.

This matter of Princess Diana's accident (over six-years ago now) and the surrounding inquiries are long overdue, and many of the general public will be pleased to hear what really happened, when it will finally be announced, if it can be believed.

It seems that many queries in regard to the French inquiry have been left open to doubt. Seemingly the CCTV Cameras had previously been turned to face the wall inside the Tunnel, and that the route was not necessary and the long way round, but why?

It seems, that the lack of a public inquiry and secrecy behind this French investigation into Diana's death has fuelled many conspiracy theories.

Like the mystery Fiat Uno hunted by French police but seemingly never found, followed by the death of a previous owner of a Fiat Uno which was at one point suspected to be the very one involved.

It has also recently been announced, that this inquest in England has been the subject of discussions and correspondence with both families (the Royals and Fayed) for some time. Seemingly these discussions and correspondence have so far not been to the satisfaction of Mr Fayed, who in the end decided to proceed on his own.

It may be fair comment to say, it's about time that something is done, and Prince Harry and William will be old enough to understand and deal with the outcome.

It has been further said or written by a Royal expert, 'I hope it will uncover a lot of things we don't already know,' but will it? It is just hoped that no one, especially the memory of poor Princess Diana will be further hurt or humiliated, by further guesswork.

What a shame that the bodyguard, Trevor Rees-Jones, who with some luck survived this accident, cannot remember more of the details surrounding it. It is common that people who have been involved in an accident come to remember most of the details after some time and we can only hope that in time his memory will return and give us all the facts, not just assumptions.

It was just recently, December 2003, when an event was thrown by the National Aids Trust (a charity created by Princess Diana) to fight HIV in Africa and other places. At the time it was formed, HIV was hardly known in this country and cases were very rare. At that time it was known mostly to occur in African countries.

This disease appears to be creeping into European and other countries now, and suddenly all Government leaders seem to have woken up to the dilemma it might cause and they now appear to have money available to try and fight it, or make themselves look great and smart again.

This appears to always be the case; allow a problem to develop, and then produce money to fight it once it is too late.

Why could this money from America and Britain not have been found many years ago, when at that time thousands upon thousands of people and infections could have been saved, and this disease could possibly have been prevented from spreading too far?

What about hunger and starvation? A problem which has been around as long as we have, let's just hope this does not spread. Not a great deal appears to have been done about this and people are allowed to die by the thousands every year, and it appears it will never be controlled. Until starvation spreads further than just the present undeveloped countries will everyone begin to wake up. Why is it that governments and leaders in prosperous countries never see things until it is too late and many more millions or billions will have to be spent, just to save a few of their own people, or themselves?

What a fine thing it would be, if the word democracy and democratic governments, supposedly run by the people for the people, could bring freedom to all, not just a few?

This however only appears to fit those at the very top. Very similar to the words 'truth' and 'facts' it would most certainly be great to have a little of these now and again from our present leadership from which ever country; what are the words again, 'Seeing is believing'; how true.

Chapter Nineteen
(Defend, Not Attack)

Since this book is all about degrading lying and, in the end, killing off fair-minded loving people, may one be allowed to go a little further on these named subjects. Most of which are combined in another book, *Might of Terror* presently being compiled and hopefully coming out at a later date.

We have just recently heard about a major attack by the American forces on the so-called terrorists in Iraq, where in many people's opinion they, and ourselves, have really no right to be; but this is another questionable matter.

Everyone should be allowed to have their own opinion, but attack, slaughter or killing without provocation is wrong; defending oneself or a country by all means, that is quite another matter.

This, the so-called largest attack since the war began, had been thought out and started by American leaders and forces, who in the end claimed victoriously to have killed 46 Iraqi Terrorists.

It was however later stated by Iraq that only about eight people had been killed and most of them ordinary civilians and children; so where are the bodies as claimed? Although even one is too many, from whichever side they may be.

I cannot help but think of one of the Iraqi Ladies with a child in her arm and others around her shouting the Americans and British out; if this is Democracy and Freedom, we all should be ashamed.

It seems once again that a great mistake has been made without United Nations Security Councils approval; it surely seems the very best thing is to get out quickly and allow Iraq to be Iraq, without force being applied.

This appears to be required and demanded now by both above named sides, but what will be different in the long run?

Oil or no oil, we in the West managed quite nicely before this vicious unprovoked attack and surely could afford to buy this stuff much cheaper than the cost of this war and subsequent rebuilding of the country; that is if we really needed it in the first place.

President George Bush of America and Prime Minister Tony Blair of Britain, just like some of the other people mentioned in this book, appear to have been allowed to go just that little too far and should not be allowed to take matters any further without approval of the UN.

But there will always be someone who believes to be above the law as everyone else and tries to dictate to others.

This, however can naturally not be said of Prince Phillip, who once again appears to have upset some people of the press over a comment made to a Sergeant Singh, an Indian policeman at the palace with a turban upon his head. Prince Phillip seemingly remarked, or asked, 'How on earth do you get that under your helmet?'[45] Quite an interestingly good gag one would have thought, but it did not seem to go down too well. Had he said this, to his own bearskin guardsmen, no doubt every would have seen it as a joke.

These days one must not or is not allowed to joke about anything connected to the beliefs of another ethnic race, especially when this guy followed on by saying he wore the turban as part of a deep felt religious belief, which was fair comment, and I believe one should be allowed to wear symbols of their belief with pride.

If one could not joke about an item of clothing without causing offence, then I feel we are going downhill faster then originally thought. Such a subtle prod of fun as Philip made here, should surely not be seen as offensive?

It has always been understood that singing, joking and laughter are the most fundamental of any society. With all the solemn and angry faces around these days, this can make quite a change and one would have thought it should be saluted, rather than held in contempt.

Could this be many people's problems? No one is prepared to crack a good joke as they are afraid this might hit the wrong note in some people's religious beliefs.

Surely God would not have minded if someone was to say, 'Do not forget your wings or you may fall down from your clouds,' or 'We shall have to buy him a set of wings before he falls from above.'

What is wrong with society, when only stern faces should be appreciated?

Chapter Twenty
(Ghost of Henry VIII)

Could this be the likely reason why spooky ghosts have been seen around a Royal Palace, would it perhaps have been the beautiful previous Princess Diana and not as assumed King Henry VIII as has recently been thought by experts?

Especially when she no doubt heard about the massive losses frittered away from her special memorial fund?

It has been written that she'd have hated to think of it lining the pockets of investors, stockbrokers and bankers, who allowed this fund to drop from £63 million down to a mere £46 million in just six years. And had this been a dog or horse, it would long have been put out of its misery, although this might be a little harsh and overstated.

It has been said that this would have broken Diana's heart, she would have wanted her money to go to people who really needed it, which one could be sure of, almost everyone could agree and would want the same.

This is a time we all have to watch our incomes, savings and outgoings, and not to expect the golden goose, or millions of pounds to fall from heaven or come our way overnight.

We, including our Exchequer, are spending or borrowing far too much, when one day the roof is going to fall down upon our heads and caution might not be a bad thing to be considered before it is too late.

This however is life today and we all have to learn, even the above mentioned, who appear to have sold its equity holdings and plans to buy safer fixed income stocks, geared to fund outgoings.

It appears the fund spokeswoman, Jo Bexley, defended the losses of The Princes Diana Fund as, 'prudent management,' this may have been well spoken, but just a little too late. One wonders if the lady, just mentioned, would have said the very same, had it been her own money?

It seems an absolute disgrace to allow other peoples money to roll down the drain, certainly not prudent management.

It is the Author's (my own) view that many people having contributed to this fund, especially the elderly, will be very disappointed when they read these details in the press and were not personally informed.

It has come to light once again, similar to the chancellor of the exchequer, spending or loosing other people's money is one of the easiest things in this life, but losing life itself, for not having enough, is quite a different matter.

One can only think about the elderly couple, recently written about who died in their own home, and all for the sake of £140 owed to British Gas for which reason they were cut off and allowed to freeze to death, just before Christmas.[46]

What a deplorable situation, especially since the matter was seemingly in the hands of Social Security, a Government organisation.

It may be fair to say that death will come to all of us sooner or later, but one hopes it will not come in such intolerable circumstances like Princess Diana's car accident, or the two elderly people mentioned a moment ago, as well as the two poor little girls from Soham, Cambridgeshire, and many others one could mention.

Or much more recent, when one of the Queen's corgi dogs was savaged, by her daughter Princess Anne's bull terrier just before the festive season.

This must have been, and surely was, heart-breaking, not only to the Queen herself, and all around, as well as any one, who appreciates love and life.

Jealousy, carelessness, sexual desires and greed, even that amongst dogs as just mentioned, can turn out to be fatal and must be very distressing, especially when these things happen suddenly and completely unexpected.

One can only feel sorry for the people and animals that have to suffer these dreadful accidents, or wilful taking of life, especially those left behind that have to suffer the consequences and heartache the rest of their lives, such as the Queen at Christmas, when she has the nation at her heart, but is also an elderly lady having lost one of her precious pet dogs, which is nothing like losing a person or child but can be almost as bad.

It seems she had already filled its special stocking and the Queen tried to help her favourite pet, but could not save it from the berserk attack, especially when her majesty had only recently been in hospital for her second knee operation in the last twelve months.

It has been stated, 'Dogs are so like their owners, a dog could almost be a substitute child,' which could be right but not always quite so simple, and, 'One cannot just let a dog go because it has behaved badly, in fact naughtiness is somehow endearing, the connection between some people and their pets may even be stronger, because animals cannot answer back, or tell tales,' which is perhaps just as well. Most dogs seem to like fighting if they happen to look at each other the wrong way, just like humans, only some are better at it.

May Her Majesty and the Royal Family as a whole, sad as it may have been at such a so–called happy time, have the forgiveness in regard to the dog's tragedy required, even if it turned out to be a sorry Christmas in 2003.

In accordance to a news programme, it seems we already have our happy Queen and Monarch back with us. It was nice to see the Queen appear beaming happily and smiling at a little girl with a bunch of flowers in front of Sandringham Church one Sunday after Christmas, shrugging off her recent worries she had with her doggies. The little girl seemingly refused to hand over the bunch of flowers to the Queen before relenting, in front of many hundreds of well-wishers. It was good to see this outstanding open smile on Her Majesties face so soon after this tragic incident, in which she had to put down one of her favourite corgi dogs, Pharos, after being savagely mauled by two of Princess Anne's bull terriers. It also seems that both of the bull terriers and the Princess have been forgiven, since it has not been fully established which of the two had been the real culprit.

May we all hope that this year, 2004, will turn out to be a happier one, for all of us including Her Majesty and the Royal Family.

★

It has been forecast that Prince Charles is likely to marry Camilla Parker Bowles, and further, that her Majesty Queen Elizabeth II, is to abdicate in 2004.[47]

Prince William appears to be thought of as 'a great King in waiting', although some people think, he may have to wait a little while yet?

As her Majesty Queen Elizabeth II announced herself some years ago, a Monarch is chosen for life, and it seems that ours is still enjoying hers.

Unforeseen circumstance may however make changes in every person's life, especially when one is not one's own master in control. Times have changed a great deal in these last few years, when unforeseen pressures formed outside may make Her Majesty change her mind. At a more senior age now, she may well prefer to relax and allow others to carry her burden of worry and concern.

The Queen's Christmas message to the nation, her latest knee operation and the loss of one of her beloved corgi dogs just before the festive season, could well play a part to forecast thoughts. However, the mauling of one of her Majesties staff, one of her longest serving maids, was to follow this incident, and involved the same bull terrier belonging to Princess Anne.[48]

On this occasion it appears that Princess Anne's three bull terriers had been confined to her rooms, which no doubt created further dog jealousy.

It seems however that, when Ruby, the 50-year-old maid, entered the room for cleaning, the dogs began yapping and barking. The woman then became frightened and ran away, with the dogs following, and one bit her leg making her scream in an agonising retreat. There appeared to have been a great deal of blood around, which did not help, but the wound appears to have been quickly cleaned and bandaged.

To savage the Queen's most cherished corgi and attack one of her longest serving housemaids in only a few days, must have been somewhat alarming to say the least. This will naturally not provide the best of relations between dogs and owners, especially when staff, are getting frightened, but facts play a great part.

At the time the housemaid Ruby thought this to be just a minor incident, and has expressed her wish for the dog not to be destroyed, and requested to retain her job and duties. However, she appears to have changed her mind in the meantime and wishes to resign after all.

Her Majesty has been under a great deal of strain and pressure lately and has been followed around by the press and media similar to the late Princess Diana. But allow us all to wait and see before making predictions of the earlier mentioned retirement.

A great deal of water will no doubt flow under bridges before her Majesty comes to a final decision.

Thoughts can often be confusing and very damaging, especially when members of serving and/or perhaps unreliable staff have expressed those thoughts.

Chapter Twenty-One
(Royal Engagements)

Every now and again it appears that the Royal Family come up for criticism from some people or media in regard to their duties or official engagements performed and remunerations received from the state.

These could be absolutely correct and should be investigated every now and again to satisfy the public, which seems for once to have been done and reported to hopefully everyone's satisfaction.

It appears, as reported, from figures compiled from the Royal Circular, that Prince Charles the eldest son and Prince of Wales has performed the most engagements in the year 2003; 494 in total. Charles was followed by Her Majesty, Queen Elizabeth II, in second place, with her public performances totalling 472. The Princess Royal totalled 455 and the poor 82 year old Duke of Edinburgh with a total of 427, which is thought to be very good, with others following down the line.

This seems quite some performance taking into consideration that there are only around three hundred and sixty five days in a year.

This surely means that often they do fulfil two public engagements in one day, cutting out weekends and holidays, this seems quite considerable, especially as many are overseas visits as well.

It would seem though, that Prince Phillip, the Duke of Edinburgh, topped the lot with a total of 578 in the previous year, when he covered thousands of miles commemorating the Queen's Golden Jubilee. How many people at his great age would be prepared to follow this record and still cracking a joke and a smile?

Congratulations to all of the Royal Family present and past, who have and are seemingly trying their very best to satisfy most of the public, if only with a constant smile, which many others often seem to forget.

No one, so far as is known, has ever recorded the days of Princess Diana, who no doubt surpassed all of the Royal Family in her days or years. No one ever seemed to have mentioned or congratulated this lady for her many honourable performances in the past, unless maybe it has been overlooked?

Speculations appear to be forever enjoyed by certain British national newspapers and other media.

It appears that the Royal Family decreed for Princess Diana's body to be embalmed before the return of her corpse from France to England. This may be quite understandable, whatever her body structural conditions, which were no doubt quite drastic, after such a massive car crash. And it was understood that the French authorities ordered these procedures, which were reasonable, considering the circumstances.

It appears however that the French or Paris police commander Jacques Mules recently insisted that these secret instructions came from London, but pointed out that this was probably decided to make the corpse more presentable, which no doubt most would understand and agree with. A great deal of rubbish once again appears to be printed by certain newspaper correspondents, which do not seem to be factual and would best be ignored since no one knows if certain persons sneaked in or out of some Palace at any time.

A great deal of hurt to many people can be circulated and brought about just for the sake of getting into print, as it is well known that newspapers just love to spread dirt if and when they can.

Guessing otherwise to Princess Diana's condition before or after this accident could be utterly disruptive, shameful and most distasteful to certain people and families who held her in high regard.

It is well known that she had qualities we most desired in a Princess as well as compassion and charisma; vulnerability and elegance; duty, beauty and love. But most of all, she was so much one of us that most felt she was one of their family.

Very few of us knew her personally, but we all of us remember her from her overwhelming and delightful pictures, glowing from every page and warming our hearts, radiating her qualities in a way that was unique.

Now after several years, it has at long last been decided to have a British inquiry into the mystery of Princess Diana's car accident after which she so tragically passed away.

There are, no doubt, many people very concerned, especially after so many serious revelations published in Paul Burrell's book about this lady, years after her departure from life. It may be helpful to some, but do we really need a further inquiry, dragging up all these painful events? And what good will it all do in the end?

It may be fair comment for some people to be concerned, especially when a name appears to have been mentioned in one of her hand written letters.

But do we not all at times when feeling low say or write things down without giving it further thought? Especially when some sort of pressure from others might be applied; why was this particular letter handed over to a servant for safekeeping?

Could this possibly have been written, while being under some certain strain or pressure, which may or could have been applied, when the lady's mind was desperately disturbed?

It seems very unlikely that a person like her husband or anyone else would even have considered a fatal accident of any kind to the mother of two sons, and these desperate thoughts must surely have been placed into her head?

This could easily have been done, without her even realising what she was doing or writing at that particular time. We all do strange things, absentmindedly, without a great deal of concern, or agree to something completely unrealistic, which we may regret having done when it is too late to change.

This could easily have been one of those occasions when she completely trusted in the person who at that particular time comforted her when feeling down and in a moment of great distress.

If we were all certain or sure of every movement in our lifetime, we would be perfect people in a perfect world. Unfortunately we are not, and every now and again we get side tracked from our own thoughts, which in such times can get tangled up like cotton wool.

Princess Diana Frances Mountbatten-Windsor was born July 1st 1961, with her latest residence given as Kensington Palace, London W8.

This person has always been known and recognised as a very sensible clear minded individual and, would almost certainly not have allowed herself to think of such evil-doings as those just mentioned without some sort of misguidance at that time, whatever the reason.

It seems that Paul Burrell, the person behind all this recent upheaval, is now saying that the newspaper pals he once trusted have now betrayed him.

This looks very much as previously written, 'That mud, which is thrown, in most cases, returns and begins to stick.'

As mentioned by Diana's previous private secretary, 'It is time people put up or shut up[49],' apart from perhaps trying to clear this ladies name. And he followed on by saying, 'All this will do no good to anyone, least of all Diana or her sons, and is going to be a very expensive waste of time and money turning out to be a farce.'

It may well be and the author of this book fully agrees, unless of course it will clear the ladies good name, which has to be cleared and once again respected.

Similar to the conspiracy theory suggesting that Princess Diana might have been pregnant and carrying Dodi's child before she died, which was allegedly confirmed by a senior French policeman. However, this has been strongly denied by the royal coroner Dr John Burton, who seemingly was present at the post-mortem.

This intervention by the coroner puts paid to the amazing story spread about earlier by Dodi's father, Mohamed Fayed, and hopefully will be struck out of any record books.

It seems that the retired coroner Dr Burton age 73, broke his silence, although somewhat strongly phrased because of the wild stories being circulated.

Dr Burton appears to have said, 'I feel sorry for her sons this is being brought up again.'[50]

Although at the time there were rumours that Princess Diana believed a beautiful brown baby girl could help unite the world, and improve relations between Muslims and Christians.

Although highly unlikely, this surely would have been a great and wonderful idea, the thought of someone such as herself the loving mother of a baby uniting different cultures, and would most certainly have been the achievement of a lifetime, if and when free to do so, which she was after the divorce had been finalised.

It appears that she had even considered a name for a child she allegedly[51] wanted to call her Allegra, an original Latin name meaning 'cheerful and full of energy'.

But would it really have been such a great idea, as she herself was given a name of a hunter – Diana was named after the Goddess of the Hunt – and was seemingly hunted down herselflf in the very end?

Chapter Twenty-Two
(My Husband)

It has recently been written, that even the two Princes, William and Harry, have decided not to meet the writer of the book called *A Royal Duty* by Paul Burrell, who they blame for the latest nightmare regarding their father Prince Charles.

They are seemingly furious that their dad was accused of wanting Princess Diana dead[52], and I imagine they do not trust ex-butler Burrell now to keep any meeting place secret.

This handwritten letter by Diana wherein the words 'My husband'[53] appear to have been mentioned, was surely written under tremendous pressure and strain, possibly even placed into her mind without allowing the lady to think straight before writing it down.

It seems however that Diana had a plan, even though it has been written that she remarked, 'Charles was a little naughty, but I still love him.'

It seems that this pretty lady continued to carry a torch for Prince Charles, but thought, 'Anything you can do, I can do better,' and no doubt was trying to tease him, which was her style from young. This unfortunately appears to have been taken out of all proportions by the press and people surrounding her and still is, which was and is a great shame. She will never now be able to rectify or justify these terrible accusations made against her

It is only hoped that most people, who knew and loved her, will have the decency to remember this fine lady as she presented herself openly when she was still alive. Now that the inquest has been opened for further investigations, it appears that some people were or are somewhat upset by some remarks. Especially regarding Dr John Burton's seemingly blunt remarks about Princess Diana's autopsy, which emphasised that she was not pregnant[54]. Although I cannot help but feel this needed to be said and brought out in the open, to satisfy certain accusations made.

It seems that some people need open remarks before they believe and in most peoples belief he was quite right in telling the truth as he saw fit.

It has been written, that if this investigation of Diana's death, alleging she was pregnant, concludes, those who have supported the process should be brought to book for wasting public money. This may be a little harsh to those who truly belief that this was no ordinary accident, especially when it was reported that the driver, who appears to have been over the drink drive limit plus drugs, had been chosen by the hotel, which seemingly belongs to the accuser.

It was said that this investigation will not stop conspiracy theorists, who will use the conclusion to further any mystery and intrigue, which may be absolutely correct, since no great person has ever been left in real peace.

Did the intelligence service, along with the British Government, play any part in Diana thinking her life was in danger? Were they indeed playing games? Or could it have been the other way round?

The coroner, in conjunction with the Metropolitan Police chief Sir John Stevens appear to have pledged to get to the truth. It is however felt that this inquiry is not what the mother of Prince William or Harry would have wanted.

It has also been made quite clear, by many people that Prince Charles and the two boys have suffered or been punished enough, without further pain to be added.

Are fantasies, facts or illusions over this car accident on August 31st 1997 becoming greater or more complicated?

It was printed in one of the national papers, how a man claims to have seen Diana's crash and claims it was no conspiracy.

It seems, that an eye witness, Mohamed Medjahdi, 29, drove in front of this big Mercedes, which to him appeared completely out of control, and he had to accelerate sharply to get away after hearing a loud crash.[55]

He saw this large black Mercedes smashing into a pillar, inside the underpass.

But reported, 'I am absolutely convinced, clear and certain, that this was a tragedy - but it was an accident.'

What about, as it was reported, the small white Uno car that was supposedly involved, leaving particles of paint on the front of the Mercedes where they seemingly collided before the crash?

And what about all the photos taken and shown in the national press to show Diana and Dodi sitting next to each other inside the Mercedes, taken from the side, possibly by someone overtaking?

But most important would be the one showing the driver and bodyguard sitting in the front seat, which must have been taken from someone in front of the car?

There, no doubt will be many more of these stories coming out, and these will have to be investigated to get to the real truth, which surely was an accident; but why and how was it caused?

It does seem strange that a person who appears to have seen it all, did not even bother to find out who and what was involved, and did not contact anyone, but stopped, sat on a bench with his girlfriend and cried. But over whom and why?

It seems that they only discovered the following morning from a friend that Princess Diana had been a passenger in this Mercedes.

How could this man possibly remember all the details, if he saw nothing else through his rear mirror, with his girlfriend sitting beside him?

Does this not seem rather strange? But surely a matter to find out as to who, and what can be believed?

It has been written, that this man Mohamed said, 'Any conspiracy would have to have been carried out by invisible men,'[56] he seems to be very certain and yet did nothing to investigate.

Referring back to the retired coroner of Richmond, South West London, and Diana's alleged pregnancy, he said he broke his silence over the post mortem because of the wild stories still circulating and added that he felt sorry for her sons that this was being brought up again. As one delighted courtier said, this will hopefully put an end to one of the conspiracy theories.

It seems, however, that Mohamed Fayed insisted that Diana and his son Dodi were murdered and accused Prince Phillip of some involvement. It appears that he raged, 'It is absolutely black and white, horrendous murder,'[57] and continued, 'I suspect not only Prince Charles,' said al Fayed, 'but also Queen Elizabeth II's husband, Philip,' whom he describes as 'racist at the core,' and added separately, 'This inquest will be a Farce.'

This the author of this book finds just a little harsh and surely overstated. Unless the good man has any further detailed evidence, he might find himself in more trouble than he bargained for, which would be of no good whatsoever.

It was written that Mr Burgess warned it could be some time before the hearing of this inquest resumes, and that Diana and Dodi's inquests may be held together.

Deputy Assistant Commissioner Alan Brown, 49, will head the team of investigators with the Met Police Commissioner Sir John Stevens in overall command.

Let us all just hope and pray that, whatever the outcome, both may be left to rest in peace without further disturbance.

May I be allowed to say, 'We all live in a beautiful, interesting world,' or as the late Queen Mother often used to say, 'What a wonderful World.' Why not allow all of us to keep it that way? If only in the name of our late very pretty and charming Princess Diana, who has had an unfortunate fatal accident and we, at long last should allow her to rest in peace.

Resting Place

Your resting-place shall be your own,
But open for the public to be shown.

Since many wish to visit you and pray,
Although they may not have a lot to say.

Those who miss, Queen Mother or Princess Di,
Allow to stand in silence have a little cry.

You are not dead; you did not die,
But glitter brightly like some stars,
High up, within, our lovely sky.

K-WA

One large headline in one of the national newspapers, *The Diatribe*, reads like a dirty tale.

It has no doubt long been known, or at least expected, that however beautiful and full of smiles this young lady Diana was, she had human feelings, just like any other woman or person in this world. Especially, since it seems, Diana knew before her wedding day the deep feelings and connections her future husband Prince Charles, the Prince of Wales, had towards another elderly female, Camilla Parker Bowles.

This strong feeling, or relationship, between these two people appears to have continued, and was possibly, not very pleasant to bear, which produced some sort of understandable envy.

It seems that Diana's sad rant at Charles and Camilla at times appeared not to help, and in the end destroyed the marriage. It seems completely out of character with Princess Diana's continually happy appearance on all occasions that she could also be so hurt within, and allowed herself to be persuaded to place her deep feelings upon tapes to be retained by so-called friends.

Furthermore, it is most distressing to find that the Metropolitan Police, who had these tapes within their control, to have allowed these to be released to some of the outsiders and what can only be described as 'Grave Robbers' of sorts, just to make a fortune.

It may be fair to say that Prince Charles and Princess Diana were divorced and thus Prince Charles could now be ruled out as a future monarch, but what about the two sons, especially Prince William who has reached the age of consent?

I cannot help but think that Princess Diana's property, whoever now owns it, should have all been allowed to go to her two sons and other family; not unscrupulous money maker's who seemingly persuaded her, to place these remarks upon tapes, in the first place. Even though these tapes themselves may have belonged to those who recorded them, they should at the very least have been cleaned or stripped with the family's permission, before returning them.

No doubt these persons could or would have had copies, but this would have been quite another matter for the courts to prevent the publicity of private or personal conversations.

It is an absolute shame and very distressing, to hear or read some of these very private and personal remarks, or maybe even complete distortions of the truth.

Could it possibly be that Prince Harry was requested to go into the depths of South Africa, Lesotho, to be away from these most hurtful announcements?

It seems that Prince Harry is wishing, and even vowed to carry on and follow into his mother's footsteps, as a caring royal.

It appears to have been said, by Prince Seisso, the younger brother of Lesotho's, King Tetsie III, that Prince Harry was carrying on from his mother, and that he wanted some role in his stay.

Prince Harry certainly appears to have enjoyed himself in Lesotho, one of the poorest countries within South Africa, which is fairly well known to my wife and I.

Prince Harry, now nineteen it seems, is going to be there for about two months during his gap year before joining the army, and wants to learn more about the AIDS problem, seeing what work is being and likely to be done and trying to tackle it.

His mother, Princess Diana, appears to have championed the AIDS cause back in the 1980s and 90s, and Harry wishes to continue her good work.

He made an impassioned plea for more help, for victims of this killer and other diseases while visiting an African orphanage, and appears to have put his back into some hard labour. As it looks from his portrayals on TV and in newspapers, he is quite happy especially with his newly cropped hairstyle, helping to plant trees and playing football with the African youngsters.

This is the only way to help underdeveloped countries and people, which I have proclaimed in my previous books. It is better to try to help the underdeveloped, by not necessarily throwing cash at them, which never appears to go to where it is wanted and needed.

Friendly personal help and assistance is a great deal more valuable to most than ignoring the poor, and pouring cash into the pockets of the rich.

Prince Harry's African mercy mission will not only help those who are in desperate need, but also those who happen to see him do his jobs, and get his hands dirty.

It has just been published recently that the secretly recorded tapes mentioned earlier have now had excerpts broadcast on the NBC network in the USA. It surely is completely wrong and should not be allowed, to have secretly recorded tapes made public, especially for financial gain? Even though the remarks made may be and are no doubt in Princess Diana's favour, especially when she felt betrayed by another woman.

All the remarks, secretly recorded back in the 1990s, were used by the writer Andrew Morton in his biography of Diana. This was after the young lady had been severely injured and killed in a car crash, and could no longer defend herself, or withdraw any permission to print.

I feel there is no doubt that I am even slightly wrong or mislead, in the assumption of certain accusations made, or conclusions drawn, some of which still appear to be shown and no doubt written about in greater detail.

But I am prepared to overlook scandal and am happy to accept the facts as have been shown and seen, facts which always speak for themselves, and louder than any, later degrading words.

No one is ever cleaner than clean, or whiter than white, even though these expressions are being used for unscrupulous and greedy advertising to catch out the unaware. The truth, however small, will inevitably always creep up to the surface in the long run. This should always be remembered, at least in regard to the dead, who have no means of defending themselves against smears or raked up dirt.

Secretly written or taped assumptions, which have seemingly been found and produced or presented at some later stage, should never be accepted as fact or proof, especially when these can no longer be corrected or defended.

There is hardly one person in this world or on this globe, who would not at some time or other make a remark, which might later be regretted.

We are, after all, only humans, who have learned certain languages for communications between ourselves, which are not always concerned with love and sweetness.

Even our Queen Elizabeth appears lately to have her problems with the security guards, walking about her private gardens or quarters with machine guns on the ready. What is the matter with this country, or what has it become or run into in these last few years?

Terrorism and hate, once created, will not automatically go away. Yes we all have to be vigilant, but there is no need to carry machine guns around everywhere.

These sorts of methods, are, or have never even been used in dictatorial countries.

In Memory

In Memory of our pretty white rose of England,
The previous Princess of Wales was loved beyond this Island.

She was adored in the Commonwealth and the whole world over,
Appearing to live with the love shown, on any four-leaf clover.

Princess Diana, loving mother, of her two sons,
Appears to have been in sorrow, and in the line of guns.

No one would ever have known the distress from her smiling face,
That she had any enemies, when showing her grace.

She was full of laughter, always showed concern,
For others to share the delight, and from her to learn.

Princess Diana married into the family of Royals,
But seemingly had very few who were really loyal.

She travelled the Commonwealth, and much of the Globe,
With much concern, friendly, loving, and full of hope.

This charming Princess, will continue to live,
In our hearts, and memory, with little to give.

K-WA

Remember Princess Diana, formerly known as Her Highness Princess Diana, Princess of Wales, when married to His Highness, Prince Charles of Wales. At that time bearing and bringing up the two boys, presently known as Prince William and Prince Harry, both seeming to resemble their mother Princess Diana, who unfortunately passed away in her early life, by virtue of a car accident.

Whatever this forced upon the British people 'New Enquiry' into the good lady's death might bring forth, she will always hopefully be remembered for her extreme care, courage, friendly and hopefulness, as well as kindness to others. A sparkling of inspiration to children and grown-ups of all ages with great care for the terminally ill and injured, always searching for peace, but was taken away in agony.

It has recently been written that the princes are said to be upset at further reports that Burrell, has added an extra muck-raking chapter to the new paperback version of his book *A Royal Duty*. May their views also be respected in memory of their fine mother the late Princess Diana.

Princess Diana's mother, Frances Shand Kydd, who was living on the Scottish Island Seil off the coast of Argyll, appeared to be in poor health, but refused to leave the Island and said, 'I wish to be buried in Oban, on the Island, I have already bought the plot.' And followed on by saying, 'I am very proud of my home, and friends,' although she seemed to be fast deteriorating, suffering from an incurable brain condition, which was expected to claim her life.

Frances Shand Kydd, born as 'Frances Ruth Burk Roche' in 1936, married the son of an Earldom, Johnnie Spencer, later 'Lord Althorp', (and the mother of our previous Princess Diana, who has now passed away after her fatal car accident in Paris, France in August 1997) has herself now passed away in Oban on the remote Scottish Isle of Seil, early June 2004.

Frances Ruth Burk Roche was born on the day King George V died, on the royal estate in Sandringham, Norfolk. Mother and daughter did not always enjoyed a happy relationship after Diana's mother ran off with wallpaper tycoon Peter Shand Kydd back in 1969. It seems that Diana's mother was heartbroken when Shand Kydd left her for a younger woman back in 1988, and she never remarried.

She seems to have been very upset when Diana died as a result of her accident, and said, 'We all expect to bury our parents but we don't expect to bury our children,' and followed on by saying, 'I've cried in public once since Diana died.' She continued by saying, 'I always felt that if I started I might never stop.'

She was really just a sad, unwell old lady who lived an isolated life on the Island Seil, off the coast of Scotland, and who suffered from Parkinson's disease. But Frances' quiet dignity after Diana died showed two things; one, where some of Diana's star quality came from; and two, that we should all end family feuds before it is too late.

Let us all just hope that mother Frances and daughter Diana meet up once more and are once again at peace together. Unfortunately, she had to pass away just one month before the permanent memorial to Diana was to be unveiled in Hyde Park, London; where she would have been guest of honour at the ceremony, even though she was not too pleased with the design. (May God bless them both).

Chapter Twenty-Three
(In Conclusion)

May I be allowed to say it is either stubborn-headed governments and leaders or some ordinary person in the street who provoke upheaval or distrust, which should be observed and controlled, since it is hardly ever those themselves, who get hurt.

It always appears to be the law-abiding citizen, who has to suffer the consequences of the above named misconstrued or provoked terrorism.

Firearms of any sort can be the consequence of serious injuries, wherever and by whomever these might be carried, and should certainly never be allowed for policing, keeping the peace and security; those are more than likely the cause.

Many people will no doubt remember when the police were used to prevent crime and assist the public, not be part of the army carrying firearms to hurt, maim or kill.

It should at all times be remembered that bad behaviour, terrorism or killing is not born into children or humans, but is, in the main, transferred by destroying, terrorising and killing others, by powerful individuals, in the first place. But to make a mockery of our Queen in one of the national newspapers, using these automatic guns for shooting down pheasants or birds, is just about the lowest level, any editor can allow him, or herself to sink, and to be shown as a cartoon, which is supposed to be funny, is an absolute disgrace.

Her Majesty had every right in saying, 'You can take that bloody thing away,' when suddenly confronted, by a policeman with a machine gun, in her private palace gardens or grounds.

The Queen, and other members, should at the very least, have been informed and made aware of what to expect.

Especially if security of the Royal Family and palace had been increased, shame upon the higher ranks in government and police officials, who have failed to do so.

It is not concrete blocks, walls and guns or heavy tanks, which keep the peace, but human understanding and willingness to talk, listen and negotiate.

Similar to, 'Snub over Wills snaps', or 'Palace bans our Arthur', and poor Arthur Edwards, royal photographer, looking down hearted and miserable after having taken some no doubt unrequested snaps recently in Switzerland of Prince William and a girl called Kate.

Arthur Edwards may well have enjoyed taking many royal photographs in the past especially of Princess Diana, Prince Charles, the Queen and Prince Phillip, but at his age, he and *The Sun* newspaper should know how and when to restrain themselves, what to show, and especially how or what to write.

Many people are no doubt very interested and curious, but not everyone, or everything, wishes to be shown or published by some individuals.

It is better in my opinion that Diana is remembered for all the good that she did, rather than the rumours and gossip. These are the memories that should persist in the nations heart, as Diana, the Princess of Wales, rests in peace.

God Bless Her

References

1 Page 9

2 Steve Dennis, 'Burrell: My Defence', *Mirror.co.uk* [online version of national newspaper], <http://www.mirror.co.uk/news/burrell/page.cfm?objectid=12340836&method=full&siteid=50143>, accessed 10 June 2004

3 Jane Kerr, 'Diana's Secret Suitors Revealed by Burrell', *Mirror,* 24 October 2004.

4 *Real Story With Fiona Bruce*, BBC 1, 27 October 2003, 7.30pm.

5 'Diana thrilled by lovers' chase', *Mirror.co.uk* [online version of national newspaper], <http://www.mirror.co.uk/news/allnews/content_objectid=13549189_method=full_siteid=50143_headline=-DIANA-THRILLED-BY-LOVERS--CHASE-name_page.html>, accessed 24 October 2003

6 Press Association, 'Burrell denies betraying Diana', *Guardian*, 27 October 2003.

7 'Queen backs William in Burrell row', *International CNN.com* [online journal], 18/9 (27 October 2003) <http://edition.cnn.com/2003/WORLD/europe/10/27/uk.burrell/>, accessed 10 June 2004.

8 Sara Nathan, 'I'll give Princes piece of my mind; Di flunkey in shocking attack on her sons', *The Sun,* 27 October 2003.

9 *Real Story With Fiona Bruce*, BBC 1, 27 October 2003, 7.30pm.

10 —

11 —

12 —

13 'Burrell denies betraying Princess', *BBC News* [online journal], (27 October 2003) <http://news.bbc.co.uk/2/hi/uk_news/3216709.stm>, accessed 10 June 2004.

14 Sara Nathan, 'I'll give Princes piece of my mind; Di flunkey in shocking attack on her sons', *The Sun,* 27 October 2003.

15 'Burrell Pounds 1/2m on US villa', *The Sun*, 30 October 2003.

16 *Richard and Judy*, Channel 4, 27 October 2003.

17 *Richard and Judy*, Channel 4, 27 October 2003.

[18] Howard Chua-Eoan, 'In living memory', *Time*, 150/11 (1997).
[19] *Diana: The Night She Died*, Channel 5, 2 November 2003, 9.00pm.
[20] 'Diana coroner tells all in bid to "stop the lies"', *Mirror.co.uk* [online version of national newspaper], <http://www.mirror.co.uk/news/allnews/page.cfm?objectid=13791657&method=full>, accessed 10 June 2004
[21] Erin Moriarty, 'Diana: Secret Documents Revealed', *CBSNEWS.com* [online journal], (21 April 2004) <http://www.cbsnews.com/stories/2004/04/20/48hours/main612794.shtml>, accessed 11 June 2004.
[22] Jane Kerr, 'Diana Letter Sensation: "They Will Try To Kill Me"', *Mirror*, 20 October 2003.
[23] Jane Kerr, 'Charles Dismisses "Servant Incident" Allegations', *Mirror*, 7 November 2003.
[24] James Saville, 'Valet George: I'm No Liar', *Sunday Mirror*, 9 November 2003.
[25] Kathryn Lister, 'Di: "Sex tape" valet a liar', *Royal Portal* [online royal journal], (18 November 2003) <http://ladydiana.portal.dk3.com/article.php?sid=1696>, accessed 14 June 2004.
[26] —

[27] Richard Littlejohn, '(Princess) Di's Revenge From Beyond the Grave', *The Sun*, 11 November 2003.
[28] Richard Littlejohn, '(Princess) Di's Revenge From Beyond the Grave', *The Sun*, 11 November 2003.
[29] 'Blair defends George Bush visit', *BBC News, World Edition* [online journal], (17 November 2003) <http://news.bbc.co.uk/2/hi/uk_news/politics/3275907.stm>, accesed 14 June 2003.
[30] Nigel Morris, 'Livingstone Says Bush is "Greatest Threat to Life on Planet"', *Independent,* 18 November 2003.
[31] Ewen MacAskill, 'Sceptical families of dead hear of "noble" cause', *The Guardian*, 21 November 2003.
[32] Trevor Kavanagh, 'Bush: I Can't Imagine the Heartbreak of Losing a Child; Exclusive', *The Sun*, 17 November 2003.
[33] 'Georgia braced for fresh rallies', *BBC News, UK Edition* [online journal], (6 November 2003) <http://news.bbc.co.uk/1/hi/world/europe/3245819.stm>, accessed 14 June 2003.

[34] 'Did We Really Land On The Moon? The Evidence', *BBC Science and Nature: Space*, <http://www.bbc.co.uk/science/space/solarsystem/earth/apolloevidence.shtml>, accessed 14 June 2004.
[35] Trevor Kavanagh, 'Operation Big Bang;Tough new laws to protect us from terrorism', *The Sun*, 24 November 2003.
[36] John McEachran, 'Sophie: My Wonderful Little Girl', *Daily Record*, 20 November 2003.
[37] Naveed Raja, 'Joyful Sophie Leaves Hospital', *Mirror*, 19 November 2003.
[38] 'Court fight over Diana tapes', *BBC News World Edition* [online journal], (3 November 2003) <http://news.bbc.co.uk/2/hi/uk_news/3237709.stm>, accessed 15 June 2004.
[39] Charles Rae, 'Queen Unveils Artwork In Shape Of, Er... Well...', *The Sun,* 22 November 2003.
[40] Clive Goodman, 'Di Crash Bungler; Exclusive', *The Sun*, 23 November 2003.
[41] —
[42] —
[43] —
[44] Mark Bolland, 'Why so many Windsors are born losers', *News of the World*, 30 November 2003
[45] Clive Goodman, 'Philip's turban insult', *News of the World*, 21 December 2003.
[46] Matthew Taylor, 'Elderly couple die after gas cut off', *The Guardian*, 23 December 2003.
[47] Ian King, 'Sun City', *The Sun*, 30 December 2003.
[48] 'Corgi's Killer Bit Maid', *Daily Record*, 31 December 2003.
[49] Patrick Jephson, 'Time They Put Up Or Shut Up', *The Sun*, 7 January 2004
[50] Jane Kerr, 'Diana Coroner Tells All In Bid To "Stop The Lies"', *Mirror*, 8 January 2004.
[51] 'Coroner: Diana Was Not Pregnant', *LondonNet* [online newsletter], (7 January 2004) <http://www.londonnet.co.uk/ln/talk/news/diana_conspiracy_news.html>, accessed 16 June 2004.
[52] Jane Kerr, 'Diana's Letter: It Was Charles', *Mirror*, 6 January 2004.
[53] —

[54] 'Diana was not pregnant – coroner', *BBC News UK Edition* [online journal], (7 January 2004) <http://news.bbc.co.uk/1/hi/uk/3376857.stm>, accessed 16 June 2004.

[55] Mark Oliver, 'Witness lends weight to Diana accident theory', *Guardian*, 16 January 2004.

[56] 'Witness: Diana crash was accident', *CNN.com* [online journal], (15 January 2004) <http://edition.cnn.com/2004/WORLD/europe/01/15/diana.witness.reut/>, accessed 16 June 2004.

[57] Jane Kerr, 'Top Cop Called In Over Charles Plot Claim', *Daily Record*, 7 January 2004.

SD - #0013 - 070726 - C0 - 197/132/8 - PB - 9781844262977 - Gloss Lamination